5

PARKING WESTBLAAK ON THE THORNICO BUILDING

Preface

Rotterdam's roofscape has a turbulent history. Most of the roofs we see today were created during or after the reconstruction following World War II. This period formed the basis of the current urban landscape – including the rooftops.

More recently, in 2008, Rotterdam became one of the first three cities in the Netherlands to set up a green roofs program to create sedum rooftops. In 2015, however, we came to the conclusion that the rooftops of Rotterdam have so much more potential. Our Multifunctional Rooftops Program provides the scope for rooftops to realise their true value: additional space in which to better enjoy life at work and at home. Rooftops have the potential to make the city more resilient and sustainable. The examples in this book are evidence of the fun that can be had.

And this is just the start. In Rotterdam, we can truly say: 'The sky is the limit'. We do not just look for solutions on the ground, but also in the air, up on the rooftops. Rotterdam has more flat roofs than any other city in the Netherlands. These flat rooftops can be used for a whole range of activities. In a busy, densely populated city, flat rooftops provide multifunctional space that is just waiting to be used.

Making better use of the rooftops is one of the ways in which our city can become resilient and climate proof. In Rotterdam, there are already more than 250,000 m² of green rooftops and 75,000 m² of solar panels. And this is just the start. Thanks to the efforts of residents, businesses and health care institutions all working together, Rotterdam will be able to take advantage of the opportunities presented by its rooftops to make the city a more attractive place in which to live and work.

Opportunities include water storage to prevent peak storm floods, harnessing solar and wind energy and creating locations for meetings as well as terraces for residents and visitors. Rooftops are made for living, working and enjoyment. There are so many interesting ideas for Rotterdam's rooftops, including student housing (rooftop villages), public rooftop parks, sports rooftops, rooftop lounges, rooftop vegetable gardens and rooftops where events can be organised. The possibilities are endless.

In September 2017, Rotterdam's Multifunctional Rooftops Program was nominated for a C40 award in the category Cities4Tomorrow. C40 is an international network of the world's megacities committed to addressing climate change. From the 174 entries, Rotterdam was one of the 25 finalists: international recognition of our efforts to improve the city! We hope that this will inspire all the people of Rotterdam and the rest of the world to look up to the sky.

AHMED ABOUTALEB
MAYOR OF ROTTERDAM

International praise

'Rotterdam is a global pioneer on resilience and adaptation. The city's Rooftops Program, nominated for a 2017 C40 Cities Award, is one of those innovative climate solutions that cities around the world should replicate. Let's keep thinking locally to act globally.'

ANNE HIDALGO, MAYOR OF PARIS AND C40 CHAIR

'The multifunctional roofscape in Rotterdam represents the holistic approach seen in many of Rotterdam's resilience projects. Through collaboration with other cities in the 100RC Network and beyond, we hope Rotterdam can inspire cities as they endeavor to build resilience to the shocks and stresses of the 21st Century.'

LINA LIAKOU, REGIONAL DIRECTOR FOR EUROPE AND MIDDLE EAST AT 100 RESILIENT CITIES

'European cities are developing innovative climate action solutions through the LIFE Programme. The Rotterdam Municipality is working with property developers and owners on the LIFE Urban Roofs project to boost investments in multifunctional roofs, which help reduce climate change impacts and reduce emissions.'

MAURO PETRICCIONE, DIRECTOR-GENERAL, DIRECTORATE GENERAL FOR CLIMATE ACTION, EUROPEAN COMMISSION

9

Introduction

Nothing makes me happier than enjoying a beautiful view. This is why I love Rotterdam so much. Every day I take pleasure from the magnificent panoramas that can be enjoyed all over the city. Starting in my own home – chosen because of its amazing views of the rooftops of Rotterdam's oldest skyscraper the Witte Huis, the Cube Houses, the Potlood block of flats, the Markthal and the Central Library. I can even see the tower of the great church, the Laurenskerk.

I am fortunate that my work also provides opportunities to enjoy such views of Rotterdam. For example, when writing my column 'The view of...' for the local Gers! Magazine. Or when showing visitors round the highest floors of The Rotterdam building complex, the penthouses of Markthal and the Timmerhuis.

When I arrange to meet friends, it is usually on a rooftop somewhere, for example Bistro Binnenrotte on the Central Library rooftop,

"Op het Dak" on the Schieblock or "The Suicide Club" on the Groot Handelsgebouw.

Naturally, I am a faithful follower of the Rotterdam Rooftop Days Festival. For a whole weekend every year in June, it is possible to visit rooftops that are normally closed to the public. The second edition coincided with the popular, temporary stairs to the rooftop of the Groot Handelsgebouw. The morning after I had climbed these stairs, I looked down on them from the rooftop of the Delftse Poort. I had been invited there to write about the rainfall radar that measures precipitation on this highest roof in the city centre. It dawned on me what a privilege it was - and is - to so frequently be able to view the city from a different perspective. For the people on the stairs opposite, being on a rooftop was probably an unusual experience.

When the idea of a book about the rooftops of Rotterdam presented itself, I was immediately enthusiastic. I could combine

my love of the city and its views with my skills as a writer and guide. The idea was that

'During the initial orientation meetings, it quickly became clear that a roof is so much more than a place to enjoy a glass of wine while viewing the skyline'

—

I would give the readers a guided tour of the city's rooftops and allow them to enjoy the beautiful views.

During the initial orientation meetings, it quickly became clear that a rooftop can be so much more than just a place to enjoy a glass of wine while viewing the skyline. For years now, the Rotterdam City Council has been working on a multifunctional rooftops program to prepare the city for the future, including rainwater retention (blue roofs), nature (green roofs), living, working and recreation (red roofs) and energy generation (yellow roofs).

As far as its rooftops are concerned, Rotterdam is an exceptional city. The city has more flat roofs than anywhere else in the Netherlands: 14.5 million m², according to figures provided by the city council. The city centre itself, rebuilt after World War II, has an incredible 1 km² of flat rooftops.

Rotterdam also leads the world when it comes to rooftop rainwater collection. Its 'Green Roofs Program' contributed to the city of Rotterdam being voted one of the 100 resilient cities - alongside megacities such as Hong Kong and Bangkok. Rotterdam is the C40 model city for climate adaptation. C40 is an international network of 92 of the world's megacities committed to addressing climate change. In September 2017, the Rotterdam City Council's plan to develop 1 km² of multifunctional rooftops in the city

centre by 2030 was nominated for a C40 award in the category Cities4tomorrow.

As you would expect from its name, this book is truly from and about Rotterdam. In its making I interviewed twenty roofing experts: all but one from Rotterdam. I also visited more than thirty rooftops in the city: blue, green, yellow and red, belonging to private individuals, homeowner associations, businesses and housing corporations. Most of the city's rooftops do not belong to the city council itself, so the enthusiastic participation and support of the roof owners is essential to achieving the council's goal of 1 km² of multifunctional rooftops, making the city a more attractive, resilient and pleasant place to live in.

The subtitle of the book 'Taking resilience to a higher level' is a deliberate reference to the fact that the topic of developing rooftops is not just of interest to Rotterdam; it is highly relevant to all the world's large cities. Efficient use of rooftops

is essential if cities are to become resilient and future-proof. The Delft University of Technology and the Rotterdam University of Applied Sciences are looking ahead and teaching students about rooftops and their potential. Rotterdam University of Applied Science's course in multifunctional rooftops encourages students from diverse backgrounds to work together right from the start to develop the rooftops of complex cities. This is essential. If we are to develop the rooftops of Rotterdam, it is imperative that ordinary people become involved and that this becomes an integral aspect of multicultural Rotterdam life. Currently, only an innovative elite is interested. Training diverse new roof specialists is a good start.

Rotterdam Rooftops is an enthusiastic, informative and, I hope, inspiring guided tour of the rooftops of Rotterdam. I full heartedly invite you to join me up on the rooftop. To enjoy the skyline and to seize new opportunities to improve the rooftops and the city. By taking individual and joint

responsibility for the development of its rooftops, we can make Rotterdam an even better place to live in and Rotterdam can continue to set the standards for the Netherlands and the world. I would love to meet you on the rooftop sometime and to enjoy the view together.

ESTHER WIENESE

'Rotterdam can continue to set the standards for the Netherlands and the world'

—

Inhoud

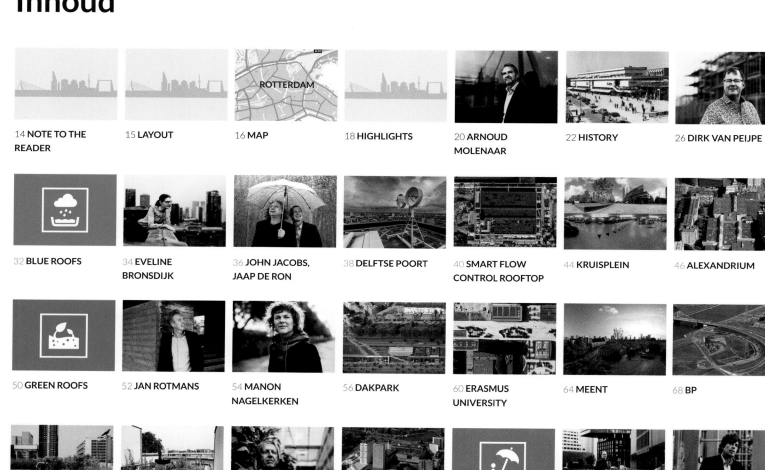

12

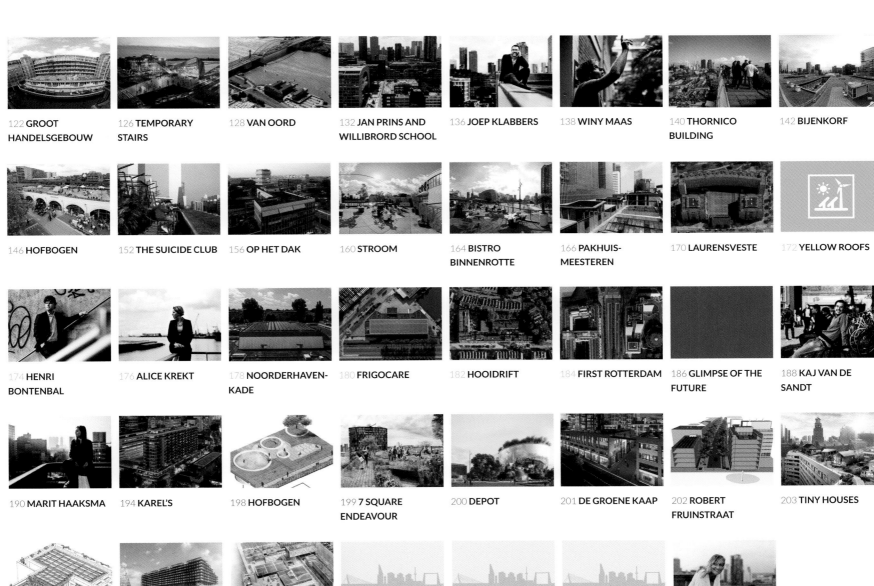

Note to the Reader

Rotterdam Rooftops is made up of three elements:

Visionaries
Experts describe the role rooftops may play in the cities of the future, each from their own perspective and point of view. Their explanations are illustrated by Marieke Odekerken's black and white portrait photos.

Example rooftops
Example rooftops demonstrate how residents, businesses and housing corporations are already using their rooftops. These rooftops have been photographed for *Rotterdam Rooftops* by:
- Chris Bonis, whose panorama photos beautifully capture the rooftops with their views of Rotterdam's skyline
- Ossip van Duivenbode, with his aerial photos showing the rooftops and the city
- Marieke Odekerken, whose photos portray character and mood

Glimpse of the future
Artist impressions of future rooftop projects offer a glimpse into the future.

Layout

Introduction

Visionaries explain the opportunities for and the necessity of developing rooftops.

Chapters

The book is divided into four separate chapters, each dedicated to a separate rooftop function. The functions are indicated by coloured stripes at the side of each page:

 Blue for rainwater buffering

 Green for gardens and nature

 Red for living, working and recreation

 Yellow for the generation of renewable energy

These functional colours and icons have been used by Rotterdam roof experts since 2015.

Each chapter starts with an introduction by two visionaries followed by descriptions of relevant example roofs. The chapters Green and Red are divided into various sub-themes, which each have their own introduction.

Multifunctional

Please note: the example rooftops are frequently multifunctional and therefore have more than one functional colour. The example rooftops are included in the chapter relevant to their most dominant function. For each rooftop, all applicable icons have been highlighted.

A13

A20

A20

VLAARDINGEN

SCHIEDAM

Nieuwe Maas

1	Delftse Poort	16	Timmerhuis
2	Smart Flow Control Rooftop	17	Montevideo
3	Kruisplein	18	Hef
4	Alexandrium	19	Jaffa Poort
5	Central Station	20	Oostplein
6	Dakpark	21	Temporary Stairs
7	Erasmus University	22	Groot Handelsgebouw
8	Meent	23	Van Oord
9	BP	24	Jan Prins and Willibrord school
10	DakAkker	25	Thornico Building
11	Mini Rooftop Farm	26	Bijenkorf
12	Erasmus Medical Centre	27	Hofbogen
13	De Karel Doorman	28	The Suicide Club
14	Didden Village	29	Op Het Dak
15	Proveniersstraat	30	Stroom

31	Bistro Binnenrotte
32	Pakhuismeesteren
33	Laurensveste
34	Noorderhavenkade
35	FrigoCare
36	Hooidrift
37	First Rotterdam
38	Karel's
39	7 Square Endeavour
40	Depot
41	Fenix 1
42	Tiny Houses
43	De Groene Kaap
44	De Heuvel

Rotterdam Rooftops - Highlights

ALEXANDRIUM SHOPPING CENTRE
THE LARGEST RENOVATED GREEN ROOFTOP IN EUROPE

HOFBOGEN
THE LONGEST ROOF IN THE NETHERLANDS

SCHIEBLOCK
THE BEST ROOFTOP IN THE NETHERLANDS
2017

DAKAKKER
THE LARGEST URBAN ROOFTOP FARM IN EUROPE

DAKPARK
THE LARGEST ROOFTOP PARK IN EUROPE

SLIMDAK
THE FIRST INTERACTIVE
SMART FLOW CONTROL
ROOFTOP IN THE
NETHERLANDS

FIRST ROTTERDAM
THE HIGHEST SOLAR
PANELS IN THE
NETHERLANDS

GROOT HANDELSGEBOUW
A PUBLIC ROOFTOP ON THE
LARGEST OFFICE BUILDING
IN THE NETHERLANDS

THE SUICIDE CLUB
THE FIRST ROOFTOP BAR
IN ROTTERDAM

**ERASMUS MEDICAL
CENTRE**
THE LARGEST ROOFTOP
GARDEN IN THE
NETHERLANDS

**ROTTERDAM
CENTRAL STATION**
THE LARGEST RAILWAY
STATION SOLAR PANEL
ROOFTOP IN EUROPE

ARNOUD MOLENAAR, CHIEF RESILIENCE OFFICER ROTTERDAM

THE RESILIENT CITY

'An integral roofscape is essential to a resilient Rotterdam'

A *resilient city* adapts to accommodate new developments such as population growth, climate change, energy transition and digitisation. 'A city such as Rotterdam needs to develop multifunctional rooftops. For several years now, as part of its climate adaptation strategy, Rotterdam has been using rooftops to collect rainwater. Large-scale integral development of its rooftops is the next step. Tremendous opportunities are there for the taking.'

Since 2014, Rotterdam has been one of The Rockefeller Foundation's *100 resilient cities*. Rotterdam was chosen because the city is a world leader in the field of climate adaptation. Arnoud Molenaar is Rotterdam's chief resilience officer. Over the coming five years, he will be responsible for initiating the integral development of the flat rooftops (1 km² in total) in the heart of the city. 'In this way, we will literally take the resilience of the city to a new level.'

Initiatives

In order to develop its rooftops, the city of Rotterdam needs the support of its residents. 'Most of the real estate in the city belongs to private individuals, homeowner associations, businesses and housing corporations. These owners are generally only interested in developing their rooftops when the roofs need replacing anyway. It is therefore important that, over the coming months and years, much attention is given to making people aware of the potential of their rooftops. Timing is vital. The number of initiatives started by the city's residents themselves is already increasing rapidly. When it comes to developing rooftops, all initiatives are more than welcome. We can all contribute to creating a resilient city.'

Eye catchers

Resilient Rotterdam focuses on the development of the 1 km² of flat rooftops in the city centre because it is in this part of the city that the greatest challenges lie. 'It is predicted that more and more people will migrate to the city and will wish to live in the city centre. The rooftops can be used for all kinds of urban functions, such as rainwater collection to prevent flooding of the streets. Solar panels and wind turbines can be installed on rooftops to make the buildings energy neutral. Plants can be grown on the rooftops to catch fine dust particles, improve air quality and reduce heat, as well as to grow food and create pleasant meeting places and parks. And of course, we can live and relax on rooftops. Rooftops become true eye catchers adding to the attractiveness of the city centre.'

Dream

In the spring of 2017, the city council received a substantial European subsidy from the LIFE program for the development of its rooftops. Together with its partners in the city, Rotterdam City Council has set up the project Life@Urban Roofs. Over the coming five years, this project will include a rooftop on which experiments can be carried out, two competitions and three rooftop projects: the Peperklip in South Rotterdam; a number of rooftops in the Robert Fruinstraat in the Middelland district (see page 202); and The Heuvel, a building on the Grote Kerkplein (see page 204). Furthermore, several initiatives for the development of the rooftops along the Lijnbaan shopping street, the Schouwburgplein (see page 199) and the Bijenkorf (see page 142) are being considered. 'These projects should be seen as stepping stones. My dream is to create a second city layer: connecting roofs to create a roofscape promenade or even an emergency exit route. After all, a resilient city needs to be safe and secure. It is unlikely that Rotterdam will flood, but not impossible. If it were to flood, then vertical evacuation, up onto the rooftops, could be the solution.'

'All initiatives for rooftops are very welcome'

—

THE TER MEULEN DEPARTMENT STORE AROUND 1952

Why are there so many flat rooftops in Rotterdam?

Rotterdam has more flat rooftops than anywhere else in the Netherlands: 14.5 million m². A logical consequence of the bombing of the inner city on the 14th of May 1940, or so you would think. However, that is just part of the story. During the research for this book, municipal historian Martin Hanning delved into the city's archives. This is his analysis.

Witte Huis

When did the first flat roof in Rotterdam appear? You would expect it to have been during the rebuilding following World War II. However, in 1898, Rotterdam already boasted a small postage stamp sized flat rooftop, amidst a sea of roof tiles, 43 metres above the ground: the lookout platform on the first skyscraper in the Netherlands, the Witte Huis (White House) in the Old Harbour. Its architect, Willem Molenbroek, was inspired by the skyscrapers of New York. Working together with contractor J.H. Stelwagen, his design marked the early beginnings of 'Manhattan on the Maas' and led to the penchant for renewal that characterises Rotterdam to this day.

Hofplein railway line

A city with such a modern office building as the Witte Huis, the tallest in Europe, naturally deserved an ultra-modern link to other cities. In 1908, the Hofplein railway line (see pages 146, 186 and 198) opened. The first electric trains in the Netherlands travelled over an enormous viaduct built from reinforced concrete: 189 arches over a length of 1900 metres. Over time, these arches have become home to an increasing number of businesses and warehouses, so this viaduct can truly be called the longest roof in Rotterdam.

Concrete

The Hofplein viaduct was designed by A.C.C.G. van Hemert and built by his own company, the Holland Reinforced Concrete Construction Company, known as the HBM. In 1910, Rotterdam was a bustling place and the use of concrete was a symbol of the new age. At least, as far as social democratic city councillor A.W. Heijkoop was concerned. He became known as Arie Beton (beton is Dutch for concrete) and with good reason: in 1916, together with Antoine Plate, he founded City Housing Corporation. Rotterdam set

about the construction of concrete social housing for the stream of new workers. The Kossel I and Kossel II districts (1921-1923, J.H. Hulsebosch) became testaments to his nickname. It was the intention that the Kiefhoek district in South Rotterdam (1925, J.J.P. Oud) would also be constructed from concrete, but the changing economic situation put a stop to that. The buildings in this district were eventually built using bricks and then plastered white. Most had flat rooftops.

The Great Depression

In the city centre, the slums with their tiled roofs were being demolished. At that time, plans were undoubtedly made for the construction of many modern buildings, such as the original Bijenkorf (1928-1930, W. Dudok). The first blocks of flats appeared, for example the Bergpolder Flat with its revolutionary steel skeletal frame (1933-1934, W. van Tijen, J.A. Brinkman and L.C. van der Vlugt). Unfortunately, because of the Great Depression, housing construction drew to a halt and then the bombing wiped out most of the centre of Rotterdam.

Districts

During the post-war reconstruction of Rotterdam, the Van Tijen Maaskant bureau was actively involved in the construction of various buildings, including the Industriegebouw on the Goudsesingel (1949), the Groot Handelsgebouw (1953) (see page 122) and the flats along the Lijnbaan (1955) (see page 194). Other parties also enthusiastically constructed large flat-roofed complexes.

All this construction work could not possibly be completed by local workers alone. Workers came from far and wide, leading to a severe housing shortage. The surrounding polders were needed to house these workers. Willem van Tijen had previously worked for the City Housing Corporation. He took the earlier idea of concrete garden villages and adapted it to form a 'district concept'. Together with young architects, this concept was realised in the form of the Zuidwijk district (1953). The first Zuidwijk district, the Horsten, was designed with sloping bitumen roofs. Zuidwijk 2, the Kampen, had flat rooftops.

Mondriaan

Architect Gerrit Rietveld was also involved in the design of the Kampen district. Together with, among others, architect Jacobus Oud and artist Piet Mondriaan, he founded De Stijl (The Style) society for fine art. De Stijl was characterised by straight lines and surfaces in primary colours. It is possible that van Tijen also brought Rietveld into contact with Lotte Stam-Beese. Her design for the Pendrecht district, combined building blocks to form a kind of mould, which she then used in the forties, fifties and sixties to fill up the empty spaces in Rotterdam. The Pendrecht district was followed by, in quick succession, Kleinpolder, Hoogvliet, the Lage Land and Ommoord. If the flat rooftops of these districts were to be painted in primary colours, an aerial photo would look like the Victory Boogie Woogie (1942-1944, Piet Mondriaan) projected onto the polder.

Systematic Building

Over the following years, flat rooftops became the rule rather than the exception, especially in the case of high-rise buildings.

In an effort to alleviate the housing shortage, fast and efficient building methods were developed. The MuWi system and the Dura-Coignet system led to the creation of great expanses of flat rooftops.

In 1964, the Van Eesteren building company started working together with the Rotterdam City Council. This led to the formation of 'The Eesteren Rational Approach', Era for short. The Era system enabled large living rooms to be created without the need for supporting dividing walls. In 1965, using this system, 624 homes were built in the Alexanderpolder. All with flat rooftops.

Urban renewal

There was yet another legacy from the past. During the seventies and eighties, many of the city centre slum dwellings that had survived the war were demolished or renovated. Frequently, the buildings that remained no longer had sloping roofs. These were sometimes replaced by whole storeys – with flat rooftops. One example of this is Jaffa, in the Kralingen district (see page 116).

Adding storeys

All this new construction meant that space on the ground became scarce. However, there were plenty of flat roofs so why not build on these? In 2001, Ibelings van Tilburg Architects looked into options for building on top of the Ter Meulen shopping centre; twelve years later this resulted in The Karel Doorman (see page 94). In 2007, Kolpa Architects added extra storeys on top of flats in and around the Kramerstraat and the De Klerkstraat in the Lage Land district.

Stimulating

The history of flat rooftops goes back much further than is discussed here, but this is not the place for a complete overview. The aim is to stimulate people to look at flat rooftops in a new light and to encourage readers to explore them, so that flat rooftops in large cities everywhere can continue to be developed, with the support and participation of the cities' residents.

ATLANTA 1938 APPROX

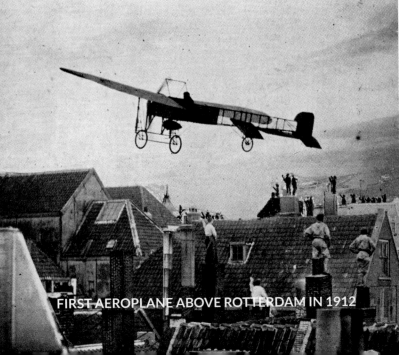
FIRST AEROPLANE ABOVE ROTTERDAM IN 1912

WITTE HUIS 1900 APPROX

DIRK VAN PEIJPE, FOUNDER OF DE URBANISTEN
THE ROTTERDAM ROOFSCAPE

'The "Rotterdam Roofscape" in one concise, visual image'

In 2015, the Rotterdam City Council contacted De Urbanisten; an innovative office for urban research, design and landscape. The Green Roofs Program was to be transformed into a multifunctional rooftop program with green, blue, red and yellow roofs. De Urbanisten were asked to present the new rooftop program through a single, appealing visual image. Dirk van Peijpe accepted the challenge. 'As long as we are given the opportunity to give it some serious thought.'

'I had long been irritated by artists' impressions of buildings and cities overgrown with vegetation', remembers Dirk. 'I call it "green porn". Pictures of trees, bushes and plants growing higgledy-piggledy on rooftops, detract from the intrinsic value and potential of the rooftops themselves. There is no ecological value in growing a mature elm on the 30th floor, even if you forget about the constructional absurdity of it. "We can do better than this", I told Paul van Roosmalen, the multifunctional rooftops program manager. "Let us consider the rooftops in their urban context".'

Roofscape

In order to explain the rooftop program in one concise image, De Urbanisten decided to explore the Rotterdam Roofscape. 'Our aim was to make the topic of rooftops in the city a popular public issue. Private individuals have their own rooftops that meet their requirements. However, most rooftops could become more colourful: red, green, yellow and blue. It doesn't have to be one or the other, colours can be combined. Looking objectively at a roofscape as a whole, you could ask yourself: what would actually be useful on high rooftops? What would be appropriate for very large rooftops? What would be preferable for rooftops in the city centre and what for rooftops in the suburbs? Such questions and their answers could lead to a plan for the whole city. People and businesses would then need to be encouraged to participate and to support it.'

Typology

Within the Rotterdam roofscape, De Urbanisten distinguished five different city types: the port, the compact city centre, the 19th century city district, the post-war city and the suburbs. 'This is an important distinction. Where is my rooftop? What characteristics does it have and what does the neighbourhood need? What makes sense where? Red roofs are especially interesting in the compact city where many people live and work and there is a lack of space. High up, some things are possible that would not be possible on the ground. The compact city also needs blue roofs because there is nowhere for the rainwater to go.'

The value of rooftops in the port areas lies in their silent, desolate vastness. 'This isolated expanse can become an ecological roofscape where birds and insects feel at home. In suburban Rotterdam, Nesselande for example, there is more than enough space and greenery at ground level. The rooftops there can be used to generate valuable renewable energy using, for example, solar panels and small wind turbines. This also applies to the blocks of flats in the post-war districts. Although on these flat rooftops, a coverage of plants can also be useful for insulation and cooling.'

Exciting

De Urbanisten have combined the wealth of rooftops and typologies in one concise image encompassing the whole city: the 19th century city districts, the suburbs, the city centre, the port, the Kop van Zuid, the iconic buildings. 'It is clearly Rotterdam. The pallet of Rotterdam's rooftops has such rich potential.'

This 'Rotterdam Roofscape', as conceived by De Urbanisten and the city council (see pages 206-207), is still valid and useful today. 'It is an in-depth, well thought out, diverse and exciting concept'.

'Consider: where is my rooftop? What are its characteristics and what does the neighbourhood need?'

PAUL VAN ROOSMALEN (LEFT), PROGRAM MANAGER MULTIFUNCTIONAL ROOFTOPS
THOD BINDER, DIRECTOR OF BINDER GROENPROJECTEN
THE VALUE OF YOUR ROOFTOP

'What is your rooftop worth?'

Faced with maintenance or renovation, why should you, as a rooftop owner, choose to install a green roof, a rooftop terrace, a rainwater storage system or solar panels? Especially when you consider that constructing a green roof, for example, costs 14-20% more than simply applying a new layer of bitumen. As far as Paul van Roosmalen, the city council's program manager Multifunctional Rooftops, and Thod Binder, director of Binder Groenprojecten, are concerned, there are countless reasons. 'Adding functionality to your rooftop can measurably increase its value.'

Paul: 'Traditionally, the most important function of a roof has always been to keep out the wind and rain. However, as early as 1923, renowned architect and urban developer Le Corbusier already questioned this: "Is it not against all logic that the uppermost layer of a city converses only with the stars?" It is certainly strange that in 2017 we think of a roof as simply being a roof and it is ridiculous that we have not done anything with the 1 km² of vacant flat rooftops in our city centre."

Sales

Nowadays project developers of new residential high-rise buildings in the city centre well realise that it pays to create green rooftops. All artists' impressions of high-rise projects flaunt green balconies and rooftop gardens. Thod has also noticed an increase in the number of inquiries at Binder Groenprojecten. "In the past, project developers were quick to scrap a rooftop garden from their design in order to cut costs, but now rooftop gardens are explicitly budgeted in. Project developers recognise that when it comes to city apartments, a rooftop garden is good for sales and increases the value of a property.'

Paul: 'In this respect, the market is maturing. In a city that is becoming more and more compact, you see that people really value their own little bit of garden or nature and are prepared to pay for it. Project developers respond to this.'

Surprised

Making existing rooftops greener is an issue that requires more attention. Paul is convinced that financial considerations are the main reason why owners simply choose to cover their rooftops with the traditional layer of bitumen. 'Everyone agrees that it is worth paying for a watertight roof. But when it comes to adding extra functionality – such as a rooftop terrace or plants – we are surprised to find that the price goes up. Costs are then calculated down to the last cent. This is not how we treat any other investment. After a year, a new car will have lost more than half its value: a terrible investment. A new kitchen is similar: its residual value is zero. But we buy these things anyway because of the values we attach to them: status, pride and pleasure.'
Thod: 'The pleasure to be had in a community rooftop garden is also of value.'

Convincing

Over the next five years, the city council

– with the support of a European LIFE-program subsidy – will set up an experimental rooftop, two competitions and three rooftop projects (see pages 20, 202 and 204). In this way, the city council will attempt to convince critics that it is worthwhile to add extra functionality to existing rooftops.

Paul: 'It is a common myth that ordinary roofs cost nothing. This is simply not true since even an ordinary roof must be maintained to prevent it leaking. When it is time to replace the roof and you have to spend 100%, why not add an extra 20%? The financial considerations will vary depending on the owner and the functions involved. Over the next five years, we are going to investigate how we can best present business cases based on the individual values for the stakeholders involved.'

Measurement

For years now, Binder Groenprojecten has been determining and substantiating the value of green roofs. Thod: 'In addition to budgeting, we judge all green projects according to the criteria of TEEB city (The Economics of Ecosystems and Biodiversity). This is an instrument set up by national government to provide

insight into the economic value (costs/ benefits) of ecosystems and biodiversity. Measurements indicate that even a relatively small investment can significantly increase the value of your rooftop. It is important that the whole lifecycle of a roof is taken into account. In other words, substantial investments need to be written off over a period of thirty years.'

'The pleasure of a community rooftop garden is also of value'

—

One of the green rooftop projects assessed by Binder Groenprojecten, using TEEB-criteria, was that of the Erasmus MC (Medical Centre) (see page 84). 'This has shown that the investment in green rooftops has led to a fivefold increase in the value of the rooftops. Of course, the Erasmus MC has thousands of square metres of green rooftop, but the same applies to even the simplest of green roofs.'

Interestingly, TEEB-measurements show

that the investor – the Erasmus MC – does not directly benefit much from the added value. 'The benefits mainly arise from a reduction in health care costs and absenteeism rates. Patients, businesses, insurance companies and the government are the main winners.'

Lower contributions

Paul: 'You would really prefer the costs to be met by those who benefit the most. The LIFE projects hope to assess who benefits and how much. This can be done by meeting and interviewing the people involved. If plants and nature are good for our health, would it be possible to translate square metres of green rooftops into lower health care contributions? Or if a building doesn't buffer rainwater, but allows it to drain away into the sewers – intended for wastewater only – can we apply the principle that the polluter pays?'

Thod: 'Furthermore, would it be a good idea if people living near a large ugly vacant black flat rooftop – of for example a shopping centre – were to contribute towards the construction of a green roof? The green rooftop of the Alexandrium Shopping Centre (see page 46) provides a much more

pleasant view for its neighbours and has reduced discomfort due to excess heat in the summer as well as muffling the noise of rain and hail. Benefits for the centre's owner include a longer life expectancy of the roof and a reduction in energy costs. In addition, the collection and buffering of rainwater by the sedum reduces peak flow to the sewers.'

Uncoupling

Paul: 'A novel idea is to switch from a 2D to a 3D land registry. Now, if you own a building, you also own the rooftop. If these two were to become uncoupled, someone else would be able to develop and exploit a rooftop or a series of rooftops. In the case of a roof such as that of the Hofbogen (see pages 146, 186 and 198), an innovative party would have already developed a High Line à la New York, attracting businesses and upgrading the neighbourhood. On top of office blocks, for example, you would be able to construct workplaces to be rented by small businesses. The people in the city have so many ideas and initiatives that it would be economically possible to develop a complete upper-city.

Rooftop business case

Financial economist Sigrid Schenk has her doubts about the direct benefits of investing in rooftops. Sigrid develops business cases for blue, green and yellow rooftops for Rebel, a financial consultancy bureau. Rebel itself owns office premises in the Oude Haven (Old Harbour) with a red and green rooftop.

What is a business case?

'A business case is a clear presentation of the costs and financial benefits of an investment. A simple business case for an investment in new functionality for a rooftop helps clarify whether such an investment is viable or not. The most important questions here are: what are the costs – including maintenance, what are the proceeds, who pays, who benefits and what are the risks?'

What about calculation tools such as TEEB?

'New functionality for rooftops, such as the generation of electricity, water buffering or rooftop gardens provides benefits such as reduction of CO_2 emissions, reduction of the likelihood of flooding or a better view. Calculation tools such as TEEB translate these into financial benefits that often exceed investment costs. However, in practice, such projects frequently remain on the drawing board: especially if no subsidies are forthcoming. The problem is that the benefits do not generally lead to financial profit for the investor.'

What is the benefit of a green rooftop?

'Green and blue roofs provide all kinds of benefits for society such as air quality improvement, rainwater buffering, reduction of heat stress and better views for adjacent premises. However, these benefits do not translate into financial profit for the owner of the premises. Financial benefits can, for example, result from better insulation and therefore reduction in energy costs for heating and cooling. Depending on the type of plants on the rooftop, the life expectancy of the roof may also increase.'

And of a blue rooftop?

'Blue rooftops can lead to reductions in the cost of water as locally collected rainwater can be recycled. However, the price of drinking water is very low so the costs of such an investment will not be recovered. The business case for a blue roof improves if social benefits – less pressure on the sewers and a reduction in the use of drinking water – are translated into financial contributions from external parties, such as the city council or the water authorities. A good example of this is the investment in water collection and reuse at the Sparta stadium (see page 37).'

What about yellow roofs?

'Private investments in solar panels are recovered within ten years, in the form of a reduction in energy costs combined with fiscal benefits. In spite of this, there are relatively few solar panels in Rotterdam. One of the main reasons is that many residents in Rotterdam do not own their own rooftops. They can only invest in solar panels through home-owner associations or housing corporations.
Even for large-scale consumers of electricity, the business case is not (yet) favourable because, in the Netherlands, the more electricity you use, the less you pay. This low price for electricity means that large-scale consumers save relatively less on their energy bills than private individuals. Because of this, the rooftops of many businesses, offices, factories, schools and shops remain empty.'

This doesn't sound encouraging.

'The trick is to combine these challenges. Residents can organise themselves into energy cooperatives to jointly invest in solar panel rooftops on businesses and industrial buildings and then use the electricity generated by these collective solar panels. This creates a feasible business case for those people of Rotterdam who do not have the possibility to install solar panels on their own roofs. The first collective solar panel rooftop set up by energy cooperative Blijstroom (see page 178) is a good example of this.'

How profitable is a red roof?

'We have a rooftop sun lounge with a restaurant and rooftop terrace for our staff. A red rooftop is no longer only found on private houses but is becoming more and more common on restaurants and offices. These use their rooftops purely for financial reasons: during construction or renovation, such a red rooftop increases the attractiveness of the premises. These investments are frequently directly profitable, so extra contributions or subsidies are not necessary. These investments also provide opportunities for adding other functionality, green and blue in particular.'

32

BLUE ROOFS

34

'"Get real" was the reaction of the people of Rotterdam'

How do you explain to the people of Rotterdam that it is essential to invest in green roofs in order to prevent flooding? Consultant Eveline Bronsdijk: 'People really had to get used to the idea that money should be invested in a green rooftop that is not only out of sight – after all it is above your head – but may also tear and leak because of the weight of the sedum plants soaking up the rainwater.' The solution was to let the roof owners experience this new phenomenon for themselves.

Rotterdam's water specialists devised the concept of green rooftops in 2008 to help counter the consequences of climate change. 'They predicted what we are now experiencing: increasingly heavy downpours, which overload the sewers. In many places in the city it is not possible to widen the sewers because, in Rotterdam, space underground is even more intensively used than above ground.'

Strategy
To solve this problem the water specialists looked to the city's 14.5 million m² of flat rooftops. Succulents and mosses on rooftops catch and collect rainwater, thereby slowing down the rate at which the water flows into the sewers. This concept formed the basis of Rotterdam's Green Roofs Program, with its aim of creating 160,000 m² of green rooftops during the period 2008-2014. Measures to achieve this goal included: communicating with rooftop owners; a green roofs subsidy; and the city council setting a good example by making its own rooftops green.

Oasis
People were not easily persuaded to invest in green rooftops and buffer water on their rooftops. '"Get real" was the reaction of the people of Rotterdam', remembers Eveline. 'After a period, the message was still not getting across, so we decided to organise information days for the roof owners, allowing them to experience a green rooftop for themselves.' The city council, together with Erwin Stam Tuinstudio, created an oasis of lemon trees, herbs, tomatoes and other plants on the roof of Bar Brasserie Engels on the Groot Handelsgebouw. For two years, on the first Sunday of every month from early spring until late autumn, Eveline was to be found there, promoting various green rooftop themes. 'On the busiest Sundays, we attracted three hundred people. At other times, only about thirty people came.' It achieved its goal. 'The trees, flowers and butterflies brought the topic of green rooftops to life. The rooftop really changed people's attitudes.'

Putting green
Wealthy residents in Kralingen and Hillegersberg were the first people to actually construct green rooftops. 'That's understandable. Despite the city's subsidy it still required a large investment.'
The following step was the realisation that it is pleasant to look out onto a green roof. 'Residents in the Lloyd district phoned to say that their neighbouring block of flats would benefit from having a green roof.'
People became more and more creative and inquired about combinations with solar panels and whether you could keep chickens on a rooftop. 'One man even asked about the best type of grass for a golf course so that he could practise putting on his rooftop.'
At one point, arguments arose in the media between people who wanted to keep pigs on their rooftop and others who considered this cruel as pigs supposedly have a fear of heights. 'At that point I realised that at last the use of rooftops had become a topical issue; the PR campaign had been successful. It is however necessary to continue providing education and information about green roofs. Over recent years the focus has shifted towards enjoyment: lounging on your rooftop terrace or pottering in your rooftop vegetable garden.'

'The green rooftop experience really changed people's attitudes'

JOHN JACOBS (LEFT), WATER SENSITIVE ROTTERDAM
JAAP DE RON, SCHIELAND AND KRIMPENERWAARD WATER AUTHORITIES
RAINWATER COLLECTION ON ROOFTOPS, VERSION 2.0

'The new standard'

Twelve years ago, sewerage management, surface water management and water purification were completely separate worlds. Now however, John Jacobs from the Rotterdam City Council and Jaap de Ron from the Schieland and Krimpenerwaard Water Authorities, together with other organisations and city residents, are seeking integral, circular solutions. 'We are going to change the world, starting with Rotterdam.'

Solution

John was one of the city council's water specialists who, twelve years ago, helped instigate 'Green Roofs' to buffer rainwater during heavy showers and so reduce the peak load on the sewers. Through his Water Sensitive concept, he is preparing Rotterdam for the future. 'Currently we are working on Green Roofs version 2.0, in which the creation of green roofs is linked in with urban development both above and below the ground. Three-dimensional concepts are super hip.'

As a representative of the water authorities, Jaap is responsible for the management of water and wastewater both above and below the ground. 'Water management begins on the rooftops. Rainwater falling on the rooftops should no longer drain straight to the streets and sewers but should be collected and used on the rooftop itself. Everyone can make intelligent use of rainwater: collect it in a water butt and use it to spray the garden during drier times. This is small-scale use, and we have some wonderful ideas for much larger scale water collection.'

'Dare to follow our wildest dreams and extend the boundaries'

—

Fresh water bubble

These ideas are being tested at several places in the city. For example, at the Sparta Stadium in the Spangen district. Rainwater falling on the stadium roof will be collected and buffered in an underground fresh water bubble. A system of pipes will enable the water to be siphoned out of the bubble and reused.

John: 'Sparta can then spray the artificial grass pitch with it. Currently the pitch is sprayed three times a day with expensive, purified tap water, even though rainwater is perfectly clean and costs nothing.'

Jaap: 'Rainwater falling on rooftops can be collected, stored and reused everywhere in the city. For example, rainwater falling on the Hofbogen in the Agniese district could be purified and reused in a spa or laundrette located in the Hofbogen below (see page 198).'

John: 'In this way, rooftops can reduce the load on the sewers and prevent flooding. By thinking multi-dimensionally, breaking through flat two-dimensional boundaries, we can literally take water management to a higher level.'

Drought

Worldwide climate change will not only lead to heavier peak showers but also to longer periods of drought and water shortage. John: 'During such dry periods it would definitely be beneficial for the Rotterdam Evides Water Company if we refrain from using valuable drinking water to spray our gardens.'

Jaap: 'In the case of the Sparta Stadium much less purified drinking water will be required to spray the pitch.'

John: 'And rainwater falling on the roof of the tram depot in Hillegersberg can be recycled to clean the trams in times when water is scarce.'

New Standard

John: 'The range of ideas is so inspiring. We need to dare follow our wildest dreams and extend the boundaries. Rotterdam is a clear world leader when it comes to water and climate adaptation. The next ambitious step has already been taken. Now it must become the new standard. The government itself must ensure that all rainwater falling on its own buildings is collected and recycled.'

John: 'Regulations could be used to force the new standard upon us, but it is better to set up new joint ventures and to actually demonstrate that it can be done. New ideas are inspiring but real impact comes from actually changing how we do things.'

Delftse Poort

In 2017 Rotterdam became the first large city in the Netherlands to have its own rain radar. This radar is located on the roof of the Delftse Poort building, the highest building in the city centre. The 40-kilometre range of the rain radar extends as far as the Hook of Holland and even some way out to sea.

The radar rotates once every minute and scans the region in 100x100 metres sections. This provides sufficient data for the water managers in Rotterdam to be able to predict exactly where in the city a shower will occur and how it will develop. Thereby en-abling the water managers to adequately regulate the water squares and underground water storage facilities in the city.

The Rotterdam Rain Radar is an initiative set up by the Rotterdam City Council, the Province of South Holland, the Hollandse Delta Water Company and the Delfland, Schieland and Krimpenerwaard Water Authorities. The unique design was developed together with Delft University of Technology. European subsidies covered half the costs.

Smart Flow Control Rooftop

—

Design: Smart Flow Control

Rooftop technology:
Optigrün Benelux

Design Smart Flow Control

Rooftop on the Schieblock:
DakAkker (Rooftop Farm)
Foundation, ZUS, Rotterdams
Milieucentrum (Rotterdam
Environment Centre) and Binder
Groenprojecten

Subsidies: CityLab010 and
Schieland and Krimpenerwaard
Water Authorities

Constructed by: Binder
Groenprojecten

Size: 120 m²

Function: test site and
demonstration rainwater storage

Completion date: spring 2018

Material: sedum, herbs, native
plants

Access: stairs from the rooftop at
the rear of the Schieblock

40

 **BEST** ROOFTOP IN THE NETHERLANDS 2017

 **FIRST** INTERACTIVE SMART FLOW CONTROL ROOFTOP IN THE NETHERLANDS

Demonstration rooftop for rainwater storage

Capturing, storing and recycling every drop of precipitation that falls on the roof. How? The new rooftop on the pavilion on the Schieblock demonstrates that it is possible. The design of the Smart Flow Control Rooftop is still under development, but this doesn't deter Jurgen Bals and Rob Luyk. 'This is the Rotterdam mentality: we don't expect the system to be perfect. We just get on with it, learning as we go and sharing our knowledge along the way.'

—

Who? Jurgen Bals, consultant urban water management with the Schieland and Krimpenerwaard Water Authorities and Rob Luyk, deputy manager Binder Groenprojecten.
Where? Schiekade
On the rooftop since? 2018
What? Water storage

41

'We want to inspire rooftop owners to make the city a more attractive place to live'

—

Why is rainwater storage on rooftops so important?

Jurgen: 'Climate change means that heavy downpours of 60 mm or more occur ever more frequently. That is the equivalent of six buckets – 60 litres – per m². If measures are not taken, streets and cellars will flood. Furthermore, the rainwater will gush through the drains into the sewers, which then become overloaded and the sludge of rainwater combined with wastewater will overflow into the canals and waterways. Not pleasant. Fortunately, there is a solution. Store the rainwater on the rooftops so it is retained until after the downpour, when the sewers can handle it. Or even better, devise ways to usefully recycle the rainwater so that it does not even need to go into the sewers.'

What is the difference between a Smart Flow Control Rooftop and a sedum rooftop that buffers rainwater?

Rob: 'A Smart Flow Control Rooftop has a much larger water storage capacity than an ordinary green rooftop. Sedum rooftops can store about 25 litres of rainwater per m² and ensure that the rainwater is retained before it eventually flows into the sewers. The Smart Flow Control Rooftop can store at least 70 litres of precipitation per m² and does not discharge any water into the sewers – except in extreme downpours when more rain falls than the system can cope with. The rainwater on the Smart Flow Control Rooftop is stored in special retaining crates. From these crates, the water can then be recycled by spraying the DakAkker (Rooftop Farm, see page 74) or potentially for flushing the toilets of the Op Het Dak restaurant (see page 156). A good example of circular engineering.'

Ideally, the water authorities would like the retaining crates on the Smart Flow Control Rooftop to be empty so that they can store all the rainwater that falls during the heaviest of downpours. The DakAkker would prefer the crates to be full so they have plenty of water for spraying their vegetable garden. How do you resolve this?'

Rob: 'The Smart Flow Control Rooftop combines these two requirements. An interactive app coupled to weather data enables the roof to act intelligently. When a heavy downpour is predicted, the roof takes action. If the predicted amount of rainfall is more than can be stored on the roof, then the retention crates are automatically emptied onto the rooftop farm. The empty crates are then ready to collect the anticipated rainwater.'

What does a Smart Flow Control Rooftop look like?

Rob: 'Green and fun. On this Smart Flow Control Rooftop, we grow sedum, herbs and native plants, amongst others. On a roof that is capable of supporting more weight you can create a vegetable garden, or a botanical garden, or even plant trees. The plants grow in a substrate layer that buffers and drains the water and provides nutrients for the plants. Below this are a dividing canvas, the retention crates to buffer the rainwater and an insulation layer. Finally, the basis is a steel roofing construction on the roof of the pavilion. We have deliberately made the Smart Flow Control Rooftop level instead of sloping in order to retain the rainwater on the roof. The overflow that building regulations obliged us to construct, will probably never be needed.'

The Smart Flow Control Rooftop is becoming the place to be to experience and learn about rainwater storage.

Rob: 'The Smart Flow Control Rooftop has an observation platform with a view of the whole rooftop. Part of the rooftop is constructed from transparent plates, making it possible to actually see the different layers of the roof. Even the drainpipes are transparent so that you can see the rainwater as it flows.'

Jurgen: 'Illustrations of cross-sections of the rooftop explaining the process are on display in the pavilion and in the hall on

the floor below. For several years now, we have been taking delegations of water experts to the underground water storage facilities beneath the Kruisplein and the Museum Park and to the water square on the Benthemplein to show them how we cope with rainwater in the city. The Smart Flow Control Rooftop has now been added to the route. This range of innovative water storage projects has reinforced Rotterdam's position as international leader in this field.'

What do you hope to achieve with this roof?'
Jurgen: 'We want to inspire all rooftop owners, whatever the size of their rooftop, to help make the city a more attractive place to live in. On the Smart Flow Control Rooftop, we can demonstrate and explain how to transform the threats posed by climate change into opportunities. For many years now, delegations from all over the world have come to the Schieblock to see how urban farming is carried out on the DakAkker. Storing rainwater and using it to spray the rooftop vegetable garden is the next step. We can really change habits and ways of thinking.'
Rob: 'We hope to change the way that both water experts and private individuals think. The average resident of Rotterdam probably still thinks: rainwater, not my

problem. But climate change is having an impact at street level. On this rooftop, we show what ordinary people can do to prevent flooding in their own environment and at the same time to increase the value of their own rooftop'.

How do people react to your message?
Jurgen: 'People like to help. This summer in the Middelland district, we set up a competition to come up with ideas for a green garden. Removing just one street tile and replacing it with one plant helps the rainwater flow through to the sub-strata. We would like to extend such initiatives to other districts and perhaps even to rooftops.'
Rob: 'The city is working on large-scale measures for water storage, but small-scale private initiatives are also useful. Garden centres already sell ready-to-use sedum packages for rooftops, but people are often worried that the roofs will start leaking. The Smart Flow Control Rooftop demonstrates how rainwater storage works and allows people to ask questions, become enthusiastic and get started.'

44

Kruisplein

Very few people are aware that the Kruisplein opposite Central Station is actually a rooftop. It is the roof of the underground Kruisplein water storage facility. The car park known as "Schouwburgplein 2" is located underneath the storage facility.

During heavy downpours, if the water level in the nearby Westersingel rises by more than ten centimetres, the excess water flows into the storage facility. Once the water level drops again, most of the water flows back into the Westersingel, of its own accord. The remaining water is discharged into the sewers. The water storage facility is then ready for the next downpour.

The Kruisplein water storage facility has a capacity of 2.4 million litres of water. This is about 20,800 bathtubs. The risk of floods in this part of Rotterdam has been significantly reduced.

The Kruisplein water storage facility was developed by the Rotterdam City Council together with the Schieland and Krimpenerwaard Water Authorities.

Alexandrium

—

Commissioned by: Corio
(now Klépierre)
Constructed by: Cazdak
Dakbedekkingen B.V. (root
suppressant roofing material) and
Binder Groenprojecten (sedum)
Size: 21,020 m²
Water buffer: maximum 770,000
litres
Access: via the offices above the
shops
Material: Optigroen roofing
system, sedum and white
reflective paint (now Optigrün)
Construction period: 2011-2013

46

A colourful water buffer

The rooftop of the Alexandrium Shopping Centre is 21,020 m², the largest renovated green rooftop in Europe. In 2011, the city council and the water authorities granted the shopping centre a subsidy for the construction of a sedum rooftop. This rooftop can delay the flow of as much as 770,000 litres of rainwater into the sewers. The sedum rooftop has also contributed to improving the attractiveness of the neighbourhood.

Who? Frenk Rozema, commercial director Cazdak Dakbedekkingen B.V.
Where? Poolsterstraat
On the roof since? 2011
What? The largest renovated green rooftop in Europe

When the bitumen roof needed renovation, why did the owner of the Alexandrium Shopping Centre choose a sedum rooftop?

'A green rooftop fits in with the image that the business wanted to portray of itself as a sustainable business.'

Did the council's green roofs subsidy influence the choice?

'Yes and no. Yes, because the city council refunded 25% of the construction costs and the water authorities contributed another 5%. No, because even with the subsidies, the green roof was more expensive than a black roof. This is mainly due to maintenance costs. A bitumen roof needs only to be swept once a year, whereas, for the maintenance of the sedum rooftop, Klépierre calls in Binder Groenprojecten up to five times a year.

The advantage of sedum is that it protects the roof from weathering and aging. Furthermore, the sedum layer, together with the white reflective plates painted on the roof, leads to a 35% reduction in the heat radiating into the shopping centre. In summer, the shopping centre is a few degrees cooler than it would otherwise be, so the air conditioning does not need to work as hard to keep the temperature agreeable.'

The neighbours were happy with the green rooftop.

'The Alexandrium is surrounded by high blocks of flats and offices. The green rooftop provides a much more attractive view for the residents and occupants. Seven different types of sedum and a flowering succulent have been planted so the colour of the roof continually changes throughout the year. That is much more interesting than looking out onto an enormous expanse of black bitumen.

People in the neighbourhood also noticed that the sedum rooftop radiated significantly less heat than the former bitumen rooftop. When I stand on the rooftop, I can feel a distinct difference in temperature between the black and the white areas of the roof. Furthermore, the sedum muffles the sound of rain and hail, so noise levels have been significantly reduced. This rooftop has definitely been good for Corio's image in this neighbourhood.'

LARGEST RENOVATED GREEN ROOFTOP IN EUROPE

47

48

Central Station

One year after the construction of Central Station had started, the decision was made to collect the rainwater falling on the railway roof and store it in an infiltration system underneath the station's bicycle park. From there, the rainwater slowly discharges into the substratum, reducing peak loads on the sewers whilst keeping groundwater levels in the Provenierswijk district sufficiently high to prevent the wooden foundations of the houses from drying out.

This is the largest solar panel station rooftop in Europe. Of the 30,000 m² of glass rooftop, 10,000 m² are used for solar panels. The 130,000 solar cells provide about 340 megawatt hours per year. More than enough energy for the station's escalators, lights and lifts. The solar panel rooftop has led to an 8% reduction in CO_2 emissions.

49

GREEN ROOFS

JAN ROTMANS, PROFESSOR OF SUSTAINABILITY TRANSITIONS AT ERASMUS UNIVERSITY
MAKING PROGRESS BY GIVING THE ROOFTOPS BACK TO THE PEOPLE

'The average person has no idea of what can be done on a rooftop'

Professor of sustainability transitions Jan Rotmans has been advocating better use of rooftops since the end of the previous century. A number of years ago, he shelved this topic. 'Developments were much too slow for my liking. I thought: it will eventually happen, but most probably not for another ten or twenty years.' Now there are signs that Rotterdam is changing. 'The roof has long been considered an endpoint: something to keep the wind and the rain out. Slowly, it is dawning on the city that a rooftop is actually a starting point with countless possibilities.'

In New York in 1995-1997, Jan discovered that a rooftop is a development platform on which you can do anything that can be done on the ground. 'My office was on the 27th floor of the United Nations Building. All kinds of things took place on the rooftops around me. They were used as foundations to build even higher. New functions appeared, such as electricity generation and urban farming. Rooftops became the scene for parties, television shoots and fashion shows. The most ravishing ladies – and gentlemen - paraded on the rooftop catwalks.'

Vivacious

If there is one city in the Netherlands that has the potential to utilise its rooftops then it is definitely Rotterdam, argues Jan. 'One, because Rotterdam has the most rooftops. Two, because it is possible to link the rooftops, thus connecting people to the buildings – regaining the human scale that was lost when high-rise buildings were constructed higgledy-piggledy throughout the city. And three, because rooftops can add to the vivacity of the city.

At first sight Rotterdam is a hard city, bleak and aloof. The rooftops could provide a "second view" of the city. The Suicide Club (see page 152) on the roof of the Groot Handelsgebouw (see page 122) is an example of such a vivacious, light-hearted place. But hardly anyone knows about it. The DakAkker (Rooftop Farm – see page 74) on the Schieblock is another example. Too few Rotterdammers know that vegetables are grown on the rooftop.'

> ## 'Slowly, it is dawning on the city that a rooftop is a starting point with countless possibilities'
>
> ---

Encouraging

Over the last eight years, in Rotterdam 100,000 m² of rooftops have been developed and made 'greener' to prevent flooding and to capture fine particle pollution. 'Rotterdam is champion of the Netherlands and international leader. However, of the total of 14.5 million m² of flat rooftops in the city, this 100,000 m² is barely 0.7%. It is an encouraging start, but do not assume that the concept of green roofs is really catching on in the city. The average person in Rotterdam has no idea of what can be done on a rooftop. In order to really make progress, we need to give the rooftops back to the people. People must be made enthusiastic by explaining why the rooftops need to be improved. Architects need to make designs showing how rooftops can contribute to a more attractive and interesting city. Legislation must be reassessed as there are no regulations for rooftops. And rooftops must become an integral part of the education of our future experts. Currently, we only use the length and breadth of the city. In 25 years, we will also use the height. Drones and flying cars will flit between the rooftops.'

MANON NAGELKERKEN, DAKPARK (ROOFTOP PARK) COORDINATOR
THE IMPORTANCE OF NEIGHBOURHOOD PARTICIPATION

'Resistance leads to better solutions'

Eighteen years ago, the residents of the Bospolder district in Rotterdam West demanded that the local disused and neglected shunting yard should be converted into a public neighbourhood park. And that they would have a say in the design of 'their' Dakpark (Rooftop Park). The Rotterdam City Council acknowledged their wishes and enjoined the project developer to cooperate. 'Our project was an environmental code project before the term was even coined.'

For the past eight years, Manon Nagelkerken has been actively involved in the Dakpark; the last two of these as coordinator of the volunteers and liaison for all parties, such as the city council, the shopkeepers and the water authority.

'If it wasn't for the local residents, the Dakpark would never have been created.' Manon well remembers the first Dakpark meeting that she attended: a brainstorming session with the theme *Art in the park*. 'At this point the local residents had been discussing the Dakpark for years. All of a sudden, a lady with a purple perm and a strong Rotterdam accent spoke up: "When can I park my arse in the grass?" Fantastic. The problem in a nutshell. That was so valuable.'

'All of a sudden a lady with a purple perm and a strong Rotterdam accent spoke up: "When can I park my arse in the grass?"'

Trust

Manon is not averse to criticism. 'On the contrary, criticism is an opportunity to jointly find positive solutions. You might find someone troublesome if they don't join in enthusiastically, but instead you could listen and appreciate their point of view. That one person probably represents ten others.'

The trick is to trust the other side, to realise that you all have the same goal: investing in a better neighbourhood. 'I well remember the time when the contractor planted the first trees and bushes. The locals who had endlessly brainstormed over the plans were keen to help with the actual planting but were initially not allowed to because the contractor was afraid that they would not do it properly. This was something I could not understand. It was their park. Also from managerial point of view I thought is would be wonderful. People would say: "I planted that tree – keep your dirty hands off".'

Resistance

The new Environmental Code will soon make this form of participation compulsory, so the knowledge gained about the local residents' participation in the Dakpark is of great interest to the city. 'If you want to develop the rooftops of the city, you will have to cooperate with, amongst others, residents and roof owners. And they want to be heard. For example, if you live on the top floor of a building and a green rooftop is constructed above you, then you want to be sure that it will not leak. Or, if someone intends to build four more stories on top of your home, then you will probably be concerned – and rightly so – about disruption during the building process and whether your balcony will still catch the sun. Fortunately, it is my experience that resistance leads to better solutions because you are forced to become more creative. As project developer, you then devise new ideas such as prefabricated flats that can be lifted onto a rooftop in one go. Or the architect comes up with a design that respects the fact that residents of the upper floors like to have and keep the feeling of living in a penthouse, a design that even improves the quality. One thing is for sure: participation is always voluntary and people like to receive something in return, in whatever form.'

Dakpark (Rooftop Park)
——

Design: Rotterdam City Council with input from local residents, Kuiper Compagnons and Sant and Co

Commissioned by: a residents' initiative in cooperation with the municipal urban development department

Constructed by: Mostert De Winter BV

Size: 8 hectares; length: almost a kilometre; breadth: 85 metres; elevation: 9 metres above ground

Function: neighbourhood park for relaxation and education

Construction period: a 15-year participation project

Completion date: 2013

Enterprising experimental rooftop

The Dakpark (Rooftop Park) Rotterdam is the first and largest public rooftop park in Europe. The Dakpark was developed with the aid of European subsidies. Resident participation was a prerequisite and that was just fine because from day one local residents demanded their say. Now that the Dakpark has been in use for four years, it is time for the next step, according to Stef Janssen, chair of the Dakpark Foundation and responsible for long-term planning: 'As far as I am concerned, this park will become a dynamic enterprising experimental rooftop.'

—

Who? Stef Janssen, visionary chair of the Dakpark Rotterdam Foundation
Where? From Marconiplein to Hudsonplein
On the roof since? The Dakpark has been in use since 2013
What? Public park

What is the Dakpark?

'The Dakpark is situated in the Bospolder/ Tussendijken district in Rotterdam West on top of the BigShops shopping boulevard on the site of a former railway yard. The park, the result of a residents' initiative, stretches for almost one kilometre and is nine metres above ground level. The local residents had devised a plan for the park long before the concept of green, blue, yellow or red roofs had been formalised. They just wanted a pleasant neighbourhood park.

The Dakpark was created thanks to local residents

'Without the efforts of local residents, the park would never have been constructed. A core group of fifty people were intensively involved for more than fifteen years: from its inception, to the final design and the actual construction. Fifteen years of cooperation with the city's department for Urban Development and the project developers. Few people enjoy the Dutch tradition of public inquiry procedures. In the case of the Dakpark, the residents took on a different role, they demanded ownership and claimed their rights as stakeholders.'

How did you get involved in the Dakpark?

'In 2012, as a rooftop innovator, I stood on the roof of the Haka building and watched the construction of the Dakpark rooftop park with awe. I realised that this was a unique process. Due to the recession, construction in the city had almost come to a standstill, yet here on a rooftop – of all places – a park was being developed. The local residents had seized their opportunity and created the necessary conditions. And they had achieved this at the most unfavourable of times.'

When you took on your position as chair of the Dakpark Foundation, did you expect it to be an easy job?

'I thought: if the residents can achieve this, the foundations for successful management must already be well in place. It turned out this was definitely not the case. A long time ago, Rotterdam City Council made efforts to bring about radical change in the field of urban development and citizen participation. But somewhere along the way, this transition stranded, despite the fact that people's activities are of great importance for the management of the environment. The urban environment cannot adapt quickly enough to keep up with the changing times. Local residents must be given the opportunity to manage things for themselves.'

You consciously call yourself "visionary chair"

'Indeed. If the Dakpark is to be further developed, then clear vision and direction are required. The classic approach to the functionality of parks, or other urban green areas, is that they should be quiet, peaceful places for relaxation and enjoyment. That is how they are constructed, and it is assumed that they will remain that way. But, if you wish to make the city greener, then you must provide a wider range of possibilities for use of these green areas. After all, a park is not a static fixed object, it is a dynamic living object. Making the city and its buildings greener should not be considered an expense but rather a profitable investment.'

How can the Dakpark become profitable?

'Dakpark Rotterdam is a good example of how the upper city could be developed. Both its citizen participation based development and its location are special. The park could fulfil a key role in the redevelopment of the fruit harbours, the economy of the neighbourhood and the increase in value of property in the area. Furthermore, it is good for self-development and job opportunities as well as for the development of infra- nature. A good example of this is the Groene Connectie, an initiative for a continuous seven-kilometre green connection around the Delfshaven district. As Dakpark Rotterdam Foundation, we aim to turn the Dakpark into a cooperative enterprise that welcomes innovative exploitation.'

How can the Dakpark be a model for the development of the upper city?

'With the help of project developers and rooftop owners, Rotterdam City Council would like to create a multifunctional upper city. Over the years, the supporters of the Dakpark have developed and further improved the rules of the game. We can and will make this knowledge available to all other citizen initiatives. The Dakpark Foundation focuses on political, managerial and professional innovation, within a decision-making culture which reassesses the division of responsibilities between local residents and the government. This creates the professional participative society that is essential if the city is to be literally and figuratively raised to a higher level.'

'A park is not a static fixed object, it is a dynamic living object'

—

Erasmus University Rotterdam

Design: different for each project

Commissioned by: Erasmus University Rotterdam

Size: sedum rooftop: currently 6,500 m², will become 14,000 m²; solar panels: currently approx. 1,400 m², will become 4,800 m²

Access: the rooftop terrace on the 4th floor of the Mandeville Building can be accessed via The Company restaurant. The Erasmus Plaza, a popular place to walk through or to sit and eat a sandwich, is actually the roof of the underground car park. The Mr. dr. K.P. van der Mandeleplein with its pond and benches is the roof of the student societies' accommodation.

Physical construction: on existing buildings

Material: various

Subsidy: € 25 per m² of sedum rooftop; SDE-subsidy for the solar panels

Campus development: 2010-2023

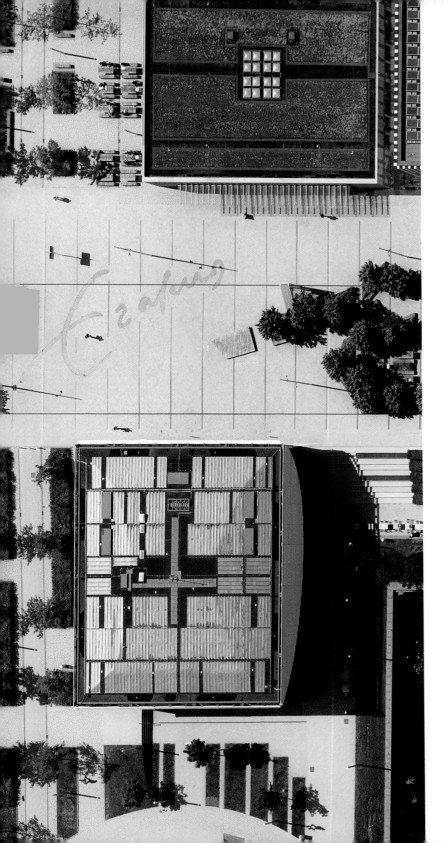

Rooftops to raise awareness

Sedum or solar panels are, or will be, installed on all the rooftops on Rotterdam Erasmus University's Woudestein campus. One of the aims of the university is to raise awareness by making sustainability visible and tangible. 'Our students and staff see the green and solar panel rooftops every time they look out of the window. We continually stimulate their environmental awareness.'

—

Who? Jan-Cees Jol, program manager Sustainability
Where? Erasmus University Rotterdam, campus Woudestein
On the roof since? 2005
What? Sedum, solar panels, green rooftop café

'It is our duty to make sure that rainwater can drain away efficiently'

—

For years now, the campus has been making use of all its rooftops. How did this come about?

'In 2010, we started the trajectory Campus in Development. Through this long-term project, lasting more than a decade, we intend to develop Woudestein into a bustling, lively and sustainable campus. Old buildings will be renovated or demolished, and new buildings will be constructed. The rooftop development process runs parallel to this.'

Why is the Erasmus University so keen on sustainable rooftops?

'Mainly because we would like to contribute to improving the environment. The campus is a built-up, stone-tiled environment. It is our duty to make sure that rainwater can drain away efficiently. Furthermore, the sedum captures fine dust particles, thereby improving air quality. The foreign students in particular think it is important that the university and campus are sustainable. It is one of the criteria by which universities are compared and chosen. A sustainable campus wins on all fronts.'

The campus has sedum rooftops.

'On the Food Plaza, on the low rooftops of the Sanders Building and the Mandeville building and on the Theil Building: in other words, on all the rooftops which are looked down upon from the other buildings. The campus is becoming greener both on the ground and in the air, thereby enhancing the green character of the campus. In December 2016, we signed a declaration of intent with the city council for the construction of an additional 10,000 m² of sedum rooftops. The first 467 m² of which are on the University Library. The rest will be planted on the Tinbergen Building, the Erasmus Building, the van der Groot Building, the Bayle Building and the new sports centre, if the latter goes ahead. A rooftop terrace will be constructed on one third of the low rooftop of the Sanders Building, the other two thirds will have a sedum covering. This is similar to the 4th floor of the Mandeville Building on which the rooftop terrace of The Company restaurant borders on a sedum rooftop.'

And the campus has solar panel rooftops.

'The flexible solar panels on the Erasmus Pavilion are glued on. They generate less energy than the permanent solar panels on the Theil Building, but have the advantage that they are lighter. This means that extra roof supports are not necessary. On the Polak Building, solar cells are incorporated into the glass parts of the roof and solar panels are installed on the rest. The students love this building because of the way the light enters the building, making it a pleasant place to study. Over the coming period, we are going to plan sedum rooftops, solar panels or combinations of these for the rooftops of existing buildings and buildings under construction.'

Do the solar panels generate enough electricity to run the campus?

'Definitely not. About 1% of the electricity that we use is generated by our own panels. The rest is 100% green wind generated energy. Over the coming three years, we aim to increase production to 4% of our consumption. However, the most important reason for constructing solar panels on the low rooftops is not to generate our own electricity. Our main aim is to encourage students and staff to become conscious of the environment. Insulation and heat storage are invisible and intangible sustainability measures. The solar panels are on view every time anyone looks out of a window.'

What about rainwater storage?

'Our sedum rooftops collect rainwater. The water then flows more slowly to the sewers, thereby reducing the flow during peak showers. The pond next to the Erasmus Pavilion also captures part of the rainwater, which then flows via an overflow into Rotterdam's open water. Over the coming years, we intend to demolish some buildings and construct a large park on the campus side of the Kralingse Zoom. This will also collect rainwater. Furthermore, we have researched possibilities for the recycling of grey water, the rainwater draining off the roofs, for example for flushing toilets. At the moment, the costs are prohibitive. But maybe it will be possible in the phase after 2020. Our aim is to have become an energy neutral campus by 2040.'

Meent Homeowners' Association

Commissioned by: Meent Homeowners' Association

Existing building: 54 homes and 18 shops in total

Size of the rooftop: a total of 2,400 m²

Size of Ingrid and Guido's rooftop terrace: 40 m²

Physical construction: wooden cantilevered joisting on brick supports

Material: treated wood, many plants and lots of compost

Access: stairs and a hydraulic trapdoor

Completion date: 2012

Contractor: Louis Buijs and Guido and Ingrid

A homeowners' association at its best

Persuading all the members of a homeowners' association to agree to a green roof is no small task. Ingrid and Guido discovered this when they found their dream rooftop in the centre of the city on a block of houses belonging to a homeowners' association. 'But we succeeded. Sedum flourishes on the whole rooftop, our rooftop terrace and that of the neighbours have been completed and three more rooftop terraces are under construction. When a maisonette comes on the market, the description now includes: with the possibility of a rooftop terrace. A pretty good achievement.'

—

Who? Ingrid Ackermans and Guido Zeck
What do they do? Ingrid is a landscape architect and the driving force behind the city's herb garden Rotterdamse Munt (Rotterdam's Mint); Guido is an architect
Where? Meent
On the roof since? 2012
What? Sedum and rooftop terraces

'We want to live in a green and pleasant city and a green roof is better for the environment'

—

How did the homeowners' association react when you said that you wanted a rooftop terrace?

'During the general members' meeting, we outlined our ideas for a rooftop terrace, sheltered from the wind and out of sight. A place where you could enjoy a glass of wine on a summer's evening, with the buzz of the city and the skyline as backdrop. A place to relax with friends at the weekend. However, it turned out that there were more important priorities. The roof needed refurbishing: it was not insulated and it leaked. Maintenance of the windows and frames was overdue and the balcony railings were rotten. We set up a technical committee there and then and got to work.'

How did you set about it?

'We invited other interested residents to meet at our house, like partners in crime. It soon became obvious that while their plans were for rooftop terraces sometime in the future, the roof itself needed to be refurbished as soon as possible. Because we want to live in a green and pleasant city and a green rooftop is better for the environment,

we looked into the pros and cons of a sedum rooftop. For the terraces, we drew up a structural analysis and submitted the plan to the city council.'

A sedum rooftop is more expensive than a bitumen rooftop. What finally persuaded the members?

'The deciding factor was that the roof was not insulated. This meant that, in winter, the maisonettes were very cold. A sedum layer insulates. The deal was that everyone contributed to the sedum, but that the maisonette owners payed for the insulation. In the end, the members voted unanimously for a green roof. Even though annual maintenance of a green roof is more expensive than an ordinary roof, despite the city council's subsidy.'

Was your professional expertise an advantage?

'Definitely. We know our way around the system. As instigators of the technical committee, we put in considerable effort to ensure that the overdue maintenance was carried out. This earned us a lot of good will,

was good for our credibility, and inspired trust. We also realised that we did not get across to some of the members because we did not properly understand each other. In these cases, we called in an expert, professionally dressed, salesman to explain things. He was able to enthuse the members that we were not able to.'

How long did it take?

'All in all, it took three years. The rooftop project was carried out at the same time as the overdue maintenance. The reason why it took such a long time was because the homeowners' association only meet once or twice a year. Just when we thought we could make a decision, it turned out that we had to go back and look into some other issue. Other problems we came across were members who were not interested or had moved to a new house or were sub-tenants and therefore had no authority. If you want to convince a homeowners' association of something, then you need to be dedicated and persistent.'

A blast resistant dune rooftop

In 2005, fifteen employees lost their lives following an explosion at the BP refinery in Texas City. 'This led to a tightening of safety and security policies worldwide: if you don't need to be at the refinery, you should not be there.' For BP Europoort this meant that new administration offices had to be constructed outside the danger zone. The futuristic roof topped with 2,500 cubic metres of earth provides protection should there ever be an explosion.

—

Who? Carlo Eijkels, Manager for Communications, Public Affairs & Government
Where? Westkant d'Arcyweg
On the roof since? 2011
What? An artificial protective dune landscape rooftop

BP

Design: GroupA
Developer: BP
Commissioned by: BP
Advice, construction and management:
Binder Groenprojecten
Material: concrete, glass, wood
Access: outside, around the building
Construction period: 2009-2011

'I am convinced that this is one of the safest buildings in the area'

—

How do you make a building blast resistant?

'This building has been built next to an artificially constructed dune valley. If an explosion should occur, the resulting pressure wave will simply roll over the building. I am convinced that this is one of the safest buildings in the area.'

Safety and security are all important to BP.

'Our philosophy is: no unnecessary risk of harm. We are constantly aware of this and keep each other alert. This includes simple rules such as all employees and visitors must hold onto the railing when going up or down the wide staircase. Basically: you leave just as healthy as you arrived'.

Danger seems so remote. From the canteen, you can't even see the refinery at all. Just nature.

'That is BP's "green" vision. This building blends in with its environment. While working on the construction plans, we heard that the Port of Rotterdam wanted to transform this area into an artificial dune landscape. We were even required to adhere to an ecological report drawn up by the building and housing inspectors.'

These were very restrictive preconditions.

'Thanks to Binder Groenprojecten it has all worked out. They are responsible for all the plants in this industrial area, know everything about rooftop gardens, and are experts on dune landscapes. Three birds with one stone. They intervened when we suggested using soil dredged from the harbour. That was definitely not the poor soil necessary for a dune landscape. The soil that is currently on top of a thick layer of sand was carefully fine-tuned to fit in with the environment. The plants on the roof merge seamlessly with the surrounding landscape.'

26,000 m² of nature reserve, including 2,600 m² of rooftop garden. That's a lot of maintenance.

'Actually, it's not so bad. Binder's dune vegetation mix has been created especially for this rooftop. It consists of various types of herbs, small trees and beautiful grass tufts whose colours change with the seasons. The plants do not grow very tall and only require manual mowing once a year. Mowing takes place strategically in the autumn, once all the seeds have dispersed. Mowing the plants just above the fallen seeds enables the roof to reseed itself.'

There are even bee hives.

'A homage to our FreeBees Saving Program. The bees are a non-aggressive Danish species so it's safe to take a walk outside. Each year they produce about forty litres of delicious honey. We also have butterflies, which are so enjoyable to watch.'

'Physically demonstrating what can be done on a rooftop is the only way'

The Rotterdams Milieucentrum (RMC – Environment Centre) would like Rotterdam to become an environment and nature friendly city and a pleasant, healthy and safe place to live. On the rooftop of the Schieblock, the RMC tests and demonstrates methods for urban farming and rainwater collection. Managing director Emile van Rinsum is internationally inspired and oriented, enthusiastic, practical and impatient. 'Just do it, is my reaction to yet another resilience congress.'

The extensive urban farm rooftops in Brooklyn, New York inspired Emile in 2011 to convert the rooftop of the Schieblock – where he had and still has his office – into the largest urban farm rooftop in Europe. The architectural firm Zus, together with the RMC, designed the DakAkker (Rooftop Farm, see page 74) and Binder Groenprojecten constructed it in 2012. Since then the DakAkker has inspired others: every year thousands of visitors and a hundred international delegations visit the rooftop. The Danes created a variation of the DakAkker in Copenhagen, the people of Brussels built an urban farming rooftop on top of the Abattoir market hall in the city's Anderlecht district and in Hong Kong a rooftop farm has been constructed on the roof of its Chinese University.

Funding

The initiators of these four urban farming rooftops have joined forces to share their knowledge about rooftop farms. One of their most important insights: urban farming on its own is not sufficiently profitable. It becomes viable only in combination with cafés, restaurants and education. 'People enjoy relaxing on a rooftop among green plants and nature. Restaurant Op het Dak (On the Rooftop, see page 156) on the DakAkker is becoming ever more popular. The Copenhagen rooftop restaurant's income is an incredible five hundred thousand euros each year. In Brussels, the plan is to serve products from the Abattoir rooftop farm together with produce from the organic market below. The urban farming rooftop in Brooklyn, with its phenomenal view of Manhattan, receives income from wedding parties. From the DakAkker, there are wonderful views of the Coolsingel and the town hall so that should also be possible here.'

'It is essential that government establishes appropriate rooftop legislation'

Rooftop flowers

The DakAkker, together with the DakGaard (Rooftop Garden) on the Hofplein station (see pages 146, 186 and 198), forms a publicly accessible testing ground for green rooftops. Experiments are carried out to discover which vegetables, fruit and edible flowers flourish on rooftops. Pesticides are not used. 'The trendsetters now farming in the city are environmentalists and use organic methods. However, urban farming will soon take off and become an important source of food for the city. Less ideologically inclined parties will become involved. It is essential that the government establishes appropriate legislation. We certainly do not want urban farmers using pesticides in the city.'

Fortifying the city

On Emile's initiative, the roof of the Schieblock has also become a testing ground for the retention and recycling of rainwater. Last winter, a Smart Flow Control Rooftop was created on the rooftop pavilion. The first intelligent water collection facility in the Netherlands. 'The computer-controlled rooftop knows when a heavy rain shower is coming and makes space in the crates that are used to spray the urban farm.' Emile invites all architects and builders to join him on the look-out plateau on the Smart Flow Control Rooftop. 'I would like all new construction projects to include water collection systems. As far as I am concerned, the government should make this compulsory. We need to fortify the city and prevent the flooding which could result from climate change. The solution is on the rooftops.'

DakAkker (Rooftop Farm)

Design: design agency ZUS
Development: ZUS, in cooperation with the Rotterdams Milieucentrum
Existing building: on the Schieblock
Commissioned by: own initiative
Constructed by: Binder Groenprojecten
Manager: DakAkker Foundation
Access: from the top floor of the Schieblock and via restaurant Op Het Dak
Awards: winner of City Initiative 2011; Rooftop Award 2017 during the Rooftop Revolution ROEF Rooftop Symposium in Amsterdam

BEST ROOFTOP IN
THE NETHERLANDS
AWARD 2017

LARGEST URBAN
FARM ROOFTOP IN
EUROPE

Officially the best rooftop in the Netherlands

The DakAkker rooftop farm on the roof of the Schieblock was already the first harvestable rooftop in the Netherlands and the largest urban farm rooftop in Europe. In September 2017, it received another accolade: The Rooftop Award 2017 for best rooftop in the Netherlands. Rooftop farmer Wouter Bauman is delighted. 'We never thought that this rooftop would receive so much attention.'

—

Who? Wouter Bauman, rooftop farmer DakAkker Foundation
Where? Schieblock
On the roof since? 2012
What? The largest rooftop vegetable garden in Europe

What is the DakAkker?

'The 1000 m² DakAkker is the largest urban farm rooftop in Europe. It is a testing ground for green rooftops. We test which vegetables, fruit, herbs and edible flowers flourish and which do not do so well on soil directly on the rooftop. We are also the test site for the Smart Flow Control Rooftop (see page 40) for the collection and recycling of rainwater.'

How did you come up with the idea of farming on the rooftop?

'In 2010, when, together with the Rotterdams Milieucentrum (RMC, Rotterdam Environment Centre), we moved into our offices in the Schieblock we looked out onto this enormous vacant expanse of black rooftop. We couldn't wait to do something with it. The design agency ZUS – who also had offices in this building – was already working on a plan for a luchtsingel (air bridge) from the Schieblock to the Hofbogen. We added the DakAkker and the DakGaard (Rooftop Orchard) on Station Hofplein (see pages 146, 186 and 198) as hotspots.

In 2011, the plan won the first City Initiative Award. With the prize money from this award and the green rooftop subsidy provided by the city council, we could make a start on our rooftop farm. It took Binder Groenprojecten only three weeks to set up the vegetable garden in 2012. Just in time for the Rotterdam International Architecture Biennale (IABR). The lettuce plants may have been rather small – but they were there. During the IABR, eighty international journalists visited the rooftop. We really had not expected that much interest. And the interest continues. Last year we welcomed nearly one hundred excursion groups, 40% of which came from abroad. In one week, our farm was visited by Flemish

> **'If you take school children to a plot of carrots and tell them to harvest them, they don't know where to start'**
>
> —

government officials, Danish landscape architects, Finish urban planners and school children from Schiedam.'

How did you end up as a rooftop farmer and what do you actually do?

'I work for the RMC as a consultant on nature and open spaces. After the construction of the DakAkker, there was no money left to hire a manager, so I took the plunge, took charge and recruited volunteers. As rooftop farmer, I am responsible for managing the rooftop; I coordinate the volunteers; supervise the summer harvesting on Friday mornings; act as beekeeper for the beehives and show delegations around. We currently have an experienced team of fifteen volunteers. They do the real work. They create this roof and are indispensable. I would never have achieved this on my own.'

Why did the DakAkker win the Rooftop Award 2017?

'Because the jury judged our rooftop to be the most attractive and the most complete. Our many edible flowers and plants, and the bees, encourage bio-diversity. The Friday harvest is served by Valerie Kuster in her rooftop restaurant Op Het Dak (see page 156) and we also sell produce to local restaurants such as De Jong, Lokaal and Esto as well as to Smakelijk Food and Drink in Vlaardingen. Local consumers mean fewer food miles.

Furthermore, during peak showers, the DakAkker currently buffers up to 60,000 litres of water and, in the spring of 2018, an innovative demonstration rooftop with a much larger rainwater storage capacity will be constructed on top of the pavilion.'

The jury also praised the opportunities for employment and social contacts.

'A number of people work in the Op Het Dak restaurant. Many of the volunteers come from the Schieblock itself or from the neighbourhood. It is a varied group: people with an office job who fancy a bit of gardening on a Friday, retired ladies, people with disabilities and the self-employed. The 130 fruit trees in the DakGaard are looked after by Binder Groenprojecten, together with volunteers. They prune the dwarf cherry, plum, apple, sweet chestnut, pear, quince and peach trees. Last year, the harvest was minimal, but we are hoping for a better one next year. We intend to work together with Jim de Jong from restaurant De Jong to put the DakGaard on the menu. I will tell him what is available for harvesting and he will devise a dish.'

Tourists find their way to the DakAkker

'Since inclusion in the Lonely Planet, we have become a real tourist attraction. Media attention has also helped. We have been the topic of many programs from the Vietnamese agricultural news to American public television, as well as Dutch radio and television shows such as gardening programs and the absolute high point: the educational children's program Het Klokhuis.'

The latter in particular was good promotion for your educational program.

'Definitely. Every Monday and Tuesday, children from junior schools in Rotterdam come here for our Dakennie children's program. Last year we welcomed more than 1200 children. Frequently, they have no more than a balcony at home. We tell them about urban farming, green roofs, healthy food and the city's bees and we set them to work. If you take them to a plot of carrots and say, "harvest time", they don't know where to start. Recently one of the children asked me "Sir, why is this the only rooftop farm in the city?" My only answer is "I don't know". I really don't know why such farms are not springing up all over this city and cities in the rest of the world.'

Mini rooftop farm

Design and construction: Binder Groenprojecten

Commissioned by: Desiree and Frank

Size: 60 m²

Subsidy: Rotterdam City Council's green roofs subsidy

Access: stairs and a glass trapdoor

Construction period: May-June 2017

78

A mini rooftop farm at home

As a child, Desiree walked hand in hand with her grandfather through his farm vegetable garden. The desire for her own vegetable garden took root and has never left her even though she has enjoyed living in urban Rotterdam for many years. A collective do-it-yourself construction project in the Nieuwe Westen district in Rotterdam made it possible to create a townhouse with a garden at the back and a vegetable garden on the rooftop. 'Growing my own vegetables in the middle of the city gives me the ultimate feeling of happiness.'

—

Who? Desiree de Baar, Frank van den Beuken and daughter Klaar
What do they do? Desiree is a visual artist and lecturer at the Willem de Kooning Academy of Art; Frank is an urban planner and strategist for the Rotterdam City Council
Where? Hooidrift
On the roof since? May 2017
What? Vegetable garden

Why have a vegetable garden on the rooftop instead of on the ground?

'My partner Frank and I came up with the idea ourselves. Frank works for the Rotterdam City Council devising resilience strategy policies. Urban farming is an aspect of this. A rooftop vegetable garden is one way of using a rooftop more efficiently. The city becomes greener, rainwater is buffered and you also grow some of your own food. As far as Frank is concerned, our roof is part of the trend towards a more sustainable city. My motivation is more personal: I am just excited about being a rooftop farmer.'

You were inspired by the DakAkker on the Schieblock

'Yes. Each week, Frank and his band practise in the rooftop pavilion on the Schieblock, so we were able to witness the DakAkker's creation and progress. When we bought this house, we discovered that the DakAkker (see page 74) had been constructed by Binder Groenprojecten. We didn't think they would be interested in such a small vegetable garden project as ours. But on the contrary, they were enthusiastic. They see this as an example rooftop for private individuals.'

And the construction?

'That was spectacular. At the end of May, an enormous crane drove up and dumped soil on the roof. Binder had calculated exactly how much weight the roof could support, with the soil spread over the pathways and beds of various depths. At the beginning of June, when everything was ready, I started sowing and planting. It was a bit late in the season, so I just kept my fingers crossed. But everything came up perfectly. Vegetables such as Chinese cabbage, artichoke, tomatoes and beans are growing well. We have already harvested delicious sweet strawberries and figs. A grape vine climbs up the wall. Herbs and flowers in the shallow beds attract the bees. Fruit bushes grow along the edges of the roof. Hopefully they will create a hedge to shelter the garden from the strong winds up here. Shortly after I had planted everything, it stormed for a few days and many plants were wrenched out of the earth – root and all.'

Who came up with the design?

'Nobody. There was no structured plan. I just planted a few things that make me happy. We intend to live here for many years yet, so I have plenty of time to discover what does and what doesn't work. For example, I discovered that tomatoes in the sun ripen more quickly than those in the shade. This is useful to know so that I can extend the harvest time.'

How do the neighbours react?

'Our neighbours all opted for solar panels

on their rooftops (see page 182), so our garden does attract attention. The people opposite, who look out on our roof, are enthusiastic and interested. A vegetable garden on the rooftop is an ideal topic for conversation because it sparks the imagination. I enjoy inviting people here. But not for long sit-down chats or to dine. We do that in the garden below. The rooftop is mainly functional. The wooden bench is only used to briefly rest and enjoy the sun between chores.'

Is a rooftop vegetable garden expensive?
'Yes, it is quite expensive. Fortunately, we received some funding from the city council's green roofs subsidy program, but we have invested a substantial sum ourselves. However, we don't begrudge a cent of it. It is such a wonderful feeling to be able to carry a few bags of seeds up onto the rooftop and come down with your arms full of home-grown vegetables.'

ALEX BURDORF, PROFESSOR OF SOCIAL HEALTHCARE AT THE ERASMUS MEDICAL CENTRE
THE EFFECT NATURE HAS ON YOUR HEALTH

'We intend to prove that it is healthy to look out onto nature'

The Erasmus Medical Centre is taking the opportunity provided by their new rooftop gardens to repeat world-renowned research into the effects of a looking out onto nature and gardens. Prof. dr. Alex Burdorf's department of Social Healthcare is going to carry out the research together with Delft University of Technology: 'Everyone would love to believe that nature and gardens are good for us, and it seems reasonable that this is the case. Even I am prepared to believe it. But I am a researcher. Belief is one thing, I need proof.'

In 1984, the Swedish dr. Roger Ulrich published an article in the prestigious journal Science Magazine, about an experiment involving forty hospital patients who had all had a major operation. Twenty of these patients were nursed in a recovery room looking out onto nature, the other twenty in a room looking out onto a brick wall. The result: the patients in the 'green' room recovered 1 to 1.5 days more quickly than those in the 'brick' room. They also needed less pain medication and experienced fewer problems such as headaches and nausea.

The article set off a worldwide movement promoting a healing environment in hospitals. 'At the Erasmus Medical Centre, we have tried to create a healing environment by ensuring there is plenty of daylight, investing in an appealing art collection and incorporating as many green areas as possible.'

Enthusiastic

Burdorf's department carries out research into health problems in various parts of the city. 'It is not easy to demonstrate conclusively, but even after taking other factors such as education, income etc. into account, there still remains an extra effect which we are not sure about. Was something wrong with our research or is it really the case that neighbourhood nature and gardens actually make people happier and therefore healthier?'

Alex is finding more and more evidence that nature is important. 'Walking through nature is calming; people become enthusiastic about blossom and autumn colours. I recently visited my upstairs neighbour whose apartment looks out onto a sedum rooftop planted by our homeowners' association on the flat roof of our apartment complex. It is a beautiful view. Furthermore, the sedum rooftop has a cooling effect on the building making it much more pleasant on sunny summer days when temperatures in the built-up city centre are up to 6°C warmer than in Nesselande, a place surrounded by plants and nature. Heat waves lasting a few days in the Netherlands always result in dozens of untimely deaths. Any city that wants its residents to enjoy a long and healthy life will need to make its rooftops green.'

Ideal

In May 2018, as soon as the nursing wards are ready in the newly constructed towers of the Erasmus Medical Centre, Alex's department will start its rerun of Ulrich's experiment. Conditions are ideal. One side of each ward looks out over the new rooftop garden; the other side onto the facade of the building opposite. Patients will spend about one week recuperating from their operation and the whole setting is new and unbiased. 'We need to carry out this experiment now. It is our window of opportunity.'

The research will be carried out blind with a minimum of 2 x 70 patients and will take about two years. 'We intend to unequivocally prove that looking out onto nature and gardens is healthier. At some point, we will publish the results.' In Science Magazine? 'That would be wonderful.'

'Any city that wants its residents to enjoy a long and healthy life will need to make its rooftops green'

83

Erasmus Medical Centre

Design: Sophia's sedum rooftops: Binder Groenprojecten; rooftop gardens and sedum rooftops on new buildings: Juurlink [+] Geluk urban development and landscape architects / EGM architects

Constructed by: Sophia: Binder Groenprojecten; rooftop gardens and new buildings: Mostert de Winter

Size: 12,000 m² of green rooftops, of which almost 3000 m² are rooftop gardens

Function: healing environment and sustainability

Construction period: 2009-2017

Completion date: rooftop gardens May 2018

Material: sedum, bamboo, pergolas, herbs, grasses and 38 wild fruit trees

Access: via the nursing ward on the 8th floor

Healing rooftop oases

Who? Liesbeth van Heel, program secretary ONE (Our New
Erasmus MC) and Margot Bleeker, fund raiser Erasmus MC
Foundation
Where? Dr. Molewaterplein
On the roof since? The two rooftop gardens will open in May 2018
What? Sedum rooftops and two rooftop gardens

Green makes everything better. Based on this philosophy, the Erasmus Medical Centre is creating green rooftops that can be viewed and two rooftop gardens where patients, their visitors and hospital employees can relax. Sponsors have donated funds to create the rooftop gardens. 'It is heart-warming that so many people are prepared to donate money for nature.'

Since 2009, the Erasmus Medical Centre has created thousands of square metres of nature on its rooftops.
Liesbeth: 'At the time, we signed a declaration of intent with the city council.

The creation of a healing environment is key to the whole philosophy behind the new construction. We hope that the nature on the rooftops will merge in with the pleasant green environment of the nearby Museum Park and Euromast Park.'

Why?
'In such a densely populated city you need green places to escape and relax. The Erasmus Medical Centre complex is a city in its own right. The complex welcomes thousands of patients and visitors daily and students and locals also come here for their shopping, meetings or for lunch. They all enjoy the many green public areas.'

Are you allowed to have plants in a hospital environment?

'You have to be very careful because of fungi, mould and other problems. Plants are therefore only allowed in the public areas. The Passage and Arcade, with their light, airy, high-ceilinged halls and bamboo plants, are very pleasant places.'

Nearly all the rooftops of the Erasmus Medical Centre are green.

'That's right. From the higher buildings, you look down on sedum rooftops. Attractive pebble patterns have been created on rooftops where there is not enough light for plants. Even that is more pleasant than looking down on ugly, vacant, black roofs. Inside, on the ground floor, the areas that have been made green are actually also rooftops: The roof of the Sophia car park has partly become a green indoor space. And the Passage, with its high green areas with plenty of daylight, is the roof of the logistics corridor.'

'It is important to have a place where you can relax and reflect'

—

The green rooftops were included right from the start of construction.

'Yes, green rooftops need to be an integral part of a construction. Otherwise, you run the risk that the rainwater soaked up by the sedum won't stay outdoors.'

The two rooftop gardens required special attention.

'Because these are accessible rooftops. Patients will be able to go, bed and all, straight from the nursing ward onto the larger of the two rooftop gardens. And there are two exits that can be used in case of an emergency evacuation. Complete Wi-Fi coverage everywhere on the rooftop was also a requirement; it is essential that employees can be contacted, and patients medically monitored.'

The rooftop gardens are well fenced off.

'The balustrade is 1.80 metres high and consists of vertical metal bars. It is attractive, transparent and easy to look through. This is very important because the railings must be safe, but not feel like a prison.'

Generous donations made construction of the rooftop gardens possible.

Margot: 'The Erasmus Medical Centre has limited budgets. Liesbeth asked if we would set up a campaign to raise funds to finance the gardens. Usually we raise money for scientific research. This is the first time that we have tackled a campaign for nature.'

How did you set about the campaign?

'Together with WWAV marketing firm, we devised a campaign which appealed to the general public. Donors could buy a cutting, a plant, a bush, a border or a tree to go in the rooftop garden. These cost between € 25 and € 10,000.'

And?

'It turned out that our message "green makes everything better" sparked the imagination. People recognised that a green environment is a healing environment and so immediately understood the positive effect that we were aiming for with our rooftop gardens.'

Who are these donors?

'The cuttings and plants were mainly bought by private individuals. Businesses and wealthy people who care about Rotterdam and the Erasmus Medical Centre were interested in procuring the trees and borders. Tree donors receive formal acknowledgement in the form of a name plate. This is the first time in the Netherlands that trees have been planted at this altitude, so it has to be seen how they fare in the wind and weather. If a tree does not survive, then we guarantee that it will be replaced by a new one.'

Did most of the donors already have links with the Erasmus Medical Centre?

'Yes. If you have been in hospital yourself, or visited a loved one here, you can understand how important it is to have a place where you can relax and reflect. Then you can surely imagine how perfect it would be to have a rooftop garden with wooden benches, wild fruit trees, pergolas, grasses and herbs to stimulate the senses. That the Erasmus Medical Centre is prepared to invest in nature is greatly appreciated. And people are proud to be able to contribute.'

Will the rooftop gardens be open to the general public?

Liesbeth: 'No. The rooftop is primarily for the patients in the hospital. They really need their peace and privacy. This cannot be combined with tourists who have, for example, just been to a museum and now want to enjoy the view from the roof.'
Margot: 'In spring 2018 we will organise a rooftop event to thank all the donors. But apart from that, the rooftop gardens will be oases for the hospital itself.'

RED ROOFS

ARJEN KNOESTER, SENIOR INNER CITY URBAN DEVELOPER
ROOFTOP PLAZA

'Look to the rooftops for green hotels, lounges and meeting places'

Currently, about 40,000 people live in the centre of Rotterdam. By 2030, this number is expected to have risen to 60,000. In order to accommodate these people, empty areas in the city are increasingly becoming built up. 'At ground level, there are fewer and smaller green areas where children can play or where one can just sit and relax on a bench. To make up for this shortage, we are increasingly looking up towards the rooftops with their boundless potential.'

Arjen Knoester, Rotterdam City Council's senior inner city urban developer, is working to ensure that the city centre remains attractive, now and in the future. 'It is important that people on the streets looking up, experience our lively, bustling city life in the same way as those on the high-rise buildings looking down. Outdoor areas, balconies and rooftop terraces are essential elements. They emphasise that people actually live in the city and at the same time provide green quality close to home. This is important because a city is not just fun. It is also an environment where it sometimes seems that a bit less concrete and asphalt would be nice'.

Liveliness

To make the city centre greener, Arjen is focussing on the vacant flat rooftops of existing buildings and newly built high-rise buildings. The residents of Rotterdam are actively helping with the rooftops of existing buildings. 'People have really started discovering the rooftops. Five years ago, we would receive about one application for a rooftop terrace each month. Now we get two or three a week. That is great, and good for the city. It is not only important that more housing is made available in the city centre, it is also essential that these houses have outdoor space.'

Meeting place

As Arjen sees it, the flat rooftops in the city provide ample potential for communal lounges and meeting places. 'In the near future, many of the residents of the city centre will live in high-rise complexes of one to three hundred apartments. It will be much more pleasant if they share more than just an entrance hall with its rows of letterboxes. People can come into contact with each other as they meet on the rooftop.

> ## 'It is great to see people coming into contact with each other as they meet on the rooftop'
>
> ---

Such a meeting place close to home is especially ideal for families. And we would like to see more people with children in the city centre because a city that is good for children is good for everyone.'

Rooftop layers

There are two separate rooftop layers in the city: the so-called Rotterdam Layer and the rooftop layer. 'The Rotterdam layer is between twenty and thirty metres above ground level on top of the six to ten storey post-war buildings. In the 2012 re-evaluation of the High-Rise Building Decree it was determined that all high-rises in the city should complement this Rotterdam Layer. In this way, a new level in the city will be created on which green areas can be created.'

The rooftop layer is formed by the rooftops of these high-rise buildings. 'People go there to rise above the busy city and to enjoy the view. We are very happy with initiatives such as the new high-rise buildings in the Zalmhaven. The future residents will have a fabulous panorama viewpoint.'

Barrier

Making the rooftops accessible for everyone or giving them a public function is not Arjen's priority. 'To be totally honest, most people think that having to walk upstairs is too much effort. People are only prepared to go skywards if there is something exciting to do there. You really have to entice them onto your rooftop.'

'Existing buildings are the perfect foundations for new buildings'

Architect Marc Ibelings, pioneer in building on top of existing buildings, is also known as the 'The godfather of Licht Verdicht'. Licht Verdicht is a recent study into the innovative construction of extra storeys on top of existing buildings in Rotterdam's city centre. 'The construction of The Karel Doorman on top of the Ter Meulen Building has demonstrated that it is definitely possible. Where there's a will, there's a way.'

It is frequently much simpler to demolish and rebuild than to restore a building. Marc: 'But each demolition erases part of a city's history. I appeal to you: if you are going to build, first take a good look at what is already there. In many cases, existing buildings form a fine foundation for new construction.'

His architectural firm Ibelings van Tilburg has demonstrated this with its restoration of the renowned Ter Meulen shopping centre (see page 22) and the construction of The Karel Doorman on the Binnenwegplein (see page 94). Based on

old photographs and drawings from 1948, the Ter Meulen building has been restored to its former glory. 'We wanted to do justice to its emotional and historic value: everyone above a certain age in Rotterdam is familiar with this post-war building.'

'Many people have never even noticed The Karel Doorman'

Sustainable
Financially, it was also sensible to preserve the building that has been standing since 1948. 'The 15,000 tonnes of concrete and stones could be reused. Not demolishing is a sustainable option: the materials are kept in function or reused and do not have to be transported long distances.'
After the renovation, two residential blocks made of 100% recyclable steel, wood, plaster

walls and glass were constructed on top of the Ter Meulen building. 'Innovative use of light material. In the Netherlands, very few residential buildings are constructed from steel. Everything is concrete, even though a steel building is six times lighter than a concrete building.'

This lighter type of building has other advantages for use in the city centre. 'Everything could be prefabricated in the factory. Complete building sections, such as balconies, could be directly hoisted from the lorries and easily fitted. There was no need for a costly, space consuming construction site. This is a huge benefit in the city centre.'

Compliment
A steel frame forms the foundation for the extra stories. 'This is a flexible open skeleton in which apartments can easily be split up or merged. The current trend is small apartments of 45 m², but in a few years, that could easily change. A building such as this can then easily be adapted.'
The facade of the residential blocks is

situated further back than the facade of the original building so the towers are not immediately noticeable from street level. 'Many people have never noticed The Karel Doorman. To me, that is a great compliment. Proof that you can increase the amount of housing in the city centre without the buildings becoming too crowded.'

Pioneering
Although The Karel Doorman has received a lot of attention, prizes and publicity, this has not led to new assignments. In order to promote the concept, Marc, together with the BNA (Royal Institute of Dutch Architects) and Rotterdam City Council, initiated the "Licht Verdicht" study. This study presents seven pioneering ideas for light construction on top of existing buildings. 'Each one is an inspirational example of notable post-war buildings on top of which extra housing could be constructed. We hope that the ideas will lead to action because you really wonder why we do not do this more often.'

De Karel
Doorman

The apartment block The Karel Doorman is located on the roof of the stately Ter Meulen building (see page 22) on the Binnenwegplein. This post-war building was designed in 1948 by Van den Broek and Bakema Architects. At that time, the enormous glass facades were revolutionary in their transparency. In 1951, the building opened its doors. It housed the Ter Meulen department store, Wassen (ladies' wear) and Van Vorst (shoes). Martin's tearoom was located on the roof of the mezzanine. In 1963, Wassen was taken over by Ter Meulen. In 1993, Ter Meulen went bankrupt and closed.

Ibelings van Tilburg architects designed the restoration of the iconic building as well as the construction of The Karel Doorman building. The new foundations support sixteen storeys, including 114 apartments and 156 parking spaces. A sheltered rooftop garden for the residents has been constructed between the two towers, 40 metres above the ground.

A sky-blue family portrait

Rooftops can be used for much more than people think. Didden Village is proof of this. Architect Winy Maas designed this mini village on the rooftop of the historic building belonging to his friends Gies and Sjoerd Didden-van de Kamp. It was the first project carried out by MVRDV architectural firm in their own city, Rotterdam, and their smallest. 'Building inspectors either approve a design, or they don't. This design was approved.'

—

Who? Ghislaine 'Gies' van de Kamp, Sjoerd Didden († 2015), owner of Studio Sjoerd Didden on the same premises, Gidius Sjoerdszoon van de Kamp and Jan Sjoerdszoon van de Kamp
Where? Beatrijsstraat
On the roof since? 2006
What? 45 m² bedrooms and 120 m² rooftop terrace

Didden Village
——

Design: MVRDV

Commissioned by: the Didden family

Existing building: a 19th century former clothing factory

Functions: 45 m² of mini village with 120 m² of rooftop terrace including two permanent picnic tables, a bench, a village square and narrow streets.

Physical construction: an iron grid on the outer wall of the roof fitted with transverse beams. Spiral stairways hang from the grid and a wooden floor has been laid on the grid.

Material: prefab construction, finished with polyurea and painted with sky blue polyurethane paint

Access: from the living room via three hanging spiral staircases

Construction period: 2005 until April 2006

Contractor: Formaatbouw BV.

Synthetic coating: KCN coating. All the sub-contractors went bankrupt during the construction crisis; staircase manufacturer Verheul is the only company to have started up again.

'The colour was love
at first sight; we never
discussed it again'

—

98

Didn't the neighbours think you were completely crazy?

'They still do. But you know, there are no rules about colours. And I still haven't come across any law decreeing that the style of a building and the construction on top of it must be from the same time period.'

Didn't anyone protest?

'Our application was publicised in the "Havenloods"; a local newspaper that, at that time, nobody read. And we didn't tell anybody. This is definitely a good tip if you are considering constructing a new rooftop: devise a plan that meets all regulations, stay as quiet as the grave until your application has been accepted and then invite all the neighbours. Nowadays, this is harder to do as all building appli-cations are listed in the Neighbourhood Alert app'.

Did you choose a sky-blue design so that it would blend in with the sky?

'The design was in this colour right from Winy's very first drawing. Sjoerd and I were immediately enthusiastic, so we never really discussed it again. I think Winy's underlying idea was that it should be in just one colour – any other colour would have done just as well – and constructed from just one material. So, no roof edges, frames or ledges. Just one smooth object. Because if you start adding details on this scale, it becomes a sort of fairy tale house.'

Why did you decide to go up onto the rooftop?

'Sjoerd Didden's atelier was and is located on the two lower floors. It houses more than 20,000 hair pieces that we design and rent out to theatres and film and television productions. We lived in the lofty rooms on the top floor. The children slept together in a garden shed that we had installed in the corner of the room. As they grew older, they wanted more privacy. When we bought this property in 1994, Winy spotted straight away that the roof would be an ideal place to build something. An idea that remained at the back of our minds.'

The contractor estimated that the construction would take three months. That became one and a half years.

'It was very naive of us to believe that the job would be completed in just three months. We just cheerfully took things as they came. If you had known beforehand that you would be camping on a building site for a year, with builders traipsing through the house at ungodly hours, leakages, no water, short circuiting, "missus – we will be on holiday for the next three weeks", a tent on the roof flapping all night, an angry neighbour fed up with the sound of sawing at 7 am... then you would just put your head in the sand and give up. But that is what is fun about life. That you do things that in retrospect you think: wow, however did I manage that?'

Do you intend to stay living here?

'I will never give this up. Sjoerd and I built this together. It is us: the house belonging to the mother and father that is a little bit higher than the children's houses; their houses are separate from ours, but still connected. It is a family portrait. Who else could live here?

'We did not tell anyone. An excellent tip when designing a new rooftop'

—

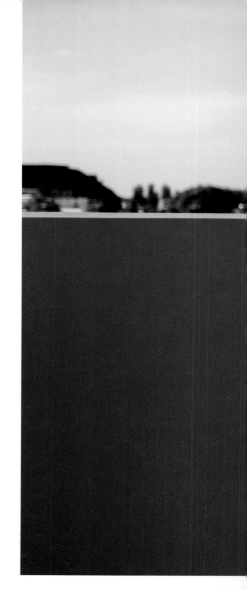

Proveniersstraat

Design: Ard Buijsen from Artisan Architects

Commissioned by: the Van Liessum family

Existing building: town house built in 1895

Function: 18 m² of rooftop lounge, 24 m² of terrace and an additional 12 m² of terrace

Material: the terrace and flower pots are made of bamboo; the building is constructed from maple wood; the sliding/tilting patio doors are aluminium (the same as in The Rotterdam and the Timmerhuis by the same manufacturer)

Licence: via the city council's (discontinued) licencing program Architect Aan Zet

Access: a new stairway

Construction period: February-May 2015

Contractor: Javi Houtbouw (javihoutbouwbv.com) recommended by the architect.

A different world

Five years ago, Richard and Marjon van Liessum were looking for a family home with a garden in the city centre. These are few and far between. So when they saw photographs of this 19th century town house with its high ceilings and stained glass windows, with just a balcony an no garden, they decided to take a look anyway. They fell in love with it, even more so when they saw the flat roof.

—

Who? Richard, Marjon and their son Sam van Liessum
What do they do? Richard is an IT-developer and manager in the financial sector.
Marjon is a biology teacher
Where? Proveniersstraat
On the roof since? 2015
What? Rooftop lounge and two terraces

'This roof is so peaceful, it invites you to relax, meditate, read and enjoy the view'

—

'It is as though the lounge wasn't placed on top of the building but grew out of it'

—

Most young parents choose to move away from the city.

'They go to Nesselande, Pijnacker or Berkel and Rodenrijs because houses there have gardens where their children can play safely. But we love the city. Sam has plenty of places to play: on the rooftop terrace, at the childcare centre, in the playground, on the nearby Zuster Hennekeplein and at his grandparents' home.'

Since last summer, Sam has his own trampoline on the rooftop.

'He loves bouncy castles so we thought a trampoline would be a good idea. It takes up a lot of space and is rather ugly but, after all, the terrace is for all three of us, including Sam. And of course, it is just temporary. When he is no longer interested, we will sell the trampoline.'

Did you have a clear plan for the roof right from the start?

'As our savings grew, so did the plans. They went from a simple fence to a green rooftop, then from part vegetable garden part terrace to this rooftop lounge. The plans for the lounge became increasingly complex. We wanted Sam to be able to play here, but also wanted enough space for a bed settee on which to relax. Furthermore, we didn't fancy continually having to carry things back and forth, so we needed a small kitchen with a fridge. And a proper staircase was definitely preferable to a trapdoor.'

Who came up with the design?

'We did. Together with the architect. The architect refers to it as a "discrete modern glass box with two terraces". From the terrace on the street side you hear the comforting buzz of the Boon Le Nord, La Cazuela and Bio Bodega terraces. The terrace at the back of the house looks out onto the facades, rooftops and gardens of the neighbouring buildings and after dark you can see the lights of the AD and Nationale-Nederlanden office blocks. This side is so peaceful. You can hear the birds singing and the wind rustling through the bamboo.'

How did you feel when the rooftop lounge was finally ready for use?

'From day one it was an integral part of the house. It has such a relaxed feel. It's as if the lounge wasn't placed on top of the house but spontaneously grew out of it. From downstairs, you look out on the neighbours and the street. Up here it's a different world; such invigorating light and colours.'

How do you use your rooftop?

'The rooftop is so peaceful: it invites you to relax and meditate, read and enjoy the view. We move with the sun or, if necessary, take shelter under our electric awning. We even celebrated New Year on our rooftop, warmed by our brazier. And since last summer we have a barbecue. This is such a special place. We are never going to leave.'

Timmerhuis

Design Timmerhuis: O.M.A. (Office for Metropolitan Architecture)

Design Terraces: Land-made garden and landscape architects

Size: 170 m² of penthouse; two rooftop terraces, each 50 m²

Function: wining & dining, jacuzzi, viewings and meetings

Construction period: 2013-2015

Material: tiles and composite decking

Access: the rooftop terrace on the 11th storey is reached via the house itself; the rooftop terrace on the 10th storey via the shared corridor

An extra rooftop terrace

Who? Danny van Munster, a Schiphol real estate developer, and Arjan Beune, deputy managing director
Where? Halvemaanpassage
On the roof since? 2015
What? Two rooftop terraces

——

Danny and Arjan are not the only ones to enjoy their penthouse in the South Tower of the Timmerhuis. Everyone is welcome. When an extra rooftop terrace at the end of the communal corridor in their penthouse came up for sale, they seized the opportunity. Since then, they begin each day quietly enjoying the red-yellow daybreak above the Markthal and end each day in their jacuzzi on the town hall side.

You weren't specifically looking for a house with a rooftop terrace.
'We were looking for a lighter, airier house with a better view and an outdoor area. The house did not necessarily have to be in Rotterdam. But, during a Sunday visit to Rotterdam, we happened to pass an advertisement for a building project on Meent street. When we saw these huge posters of homes with rooftop terraces it was love at first sight. A few days later we came back for a proper look.'

And the penthouse was still for sale?
'Yes. Luckily for us, it was during the economic recession. Many people feared losing their jobs, the housing market was at a standstill and house prices were relatively

low. We were able to afford it because we both had a good job and we don't have any children. We would not be able to afford it now. Some of our neighbours have sold their homes at a 30% profit.'

You freely allow others to enjoy your penthouse and rooftop terraces.

'It is so fantastic here that we love to share. During the week, and nearly every weekend, family and friends come to visit. And lots of children: they especially love the jacuzzi on the 10th floor rooftop terrace. Access to that terrace is from the communal corridor. All those people walking through the corridor in dressing gowns, swimming costumes and flip-flops is an amusing sight.'

How did you manage to acquire this extra terrace?

'It is the only rooftop of the building that does not directly border on an apartment. The developer had offered it to various neighbours, but they were not interested. When it threatened to become an anonymous rooftop terrace belonging to the homeowners' association, we decided to step in. The rooftop terrace is close to our bedroom so we thought it would be better if we were the ones responsible for holding rooftop parties there.'

And the idea for the jacuzzi?

'A jacuzzi provides us with a good reason to go to that terrace. After all, we have to leave our house to get there. The inflatable Jacuzzi is a relatively simple and affordable experiment. The terrace itself does not have running water. So when we put the tub outside in the spring and when it needs cleaning, we have to use a thirty-metre hosepipe running through the corridor to fill it. When the summer comes to an end, we empty and deflate the bath, fold it up and store it downstairs in the storage room.'

The terrace with the jacuzzi is in Ibiza style; the penthouse terrace is in the style of the New York High Line park.

'We came up with this idea together with the designer. The Ibiza terrace boasts a large sofa in azure-blue shades, perfect for lounging in the sun. Ideally, there would also be a pergola covered with white fabrics, lightly flapping in the breeze. Because there is no running water on this terrace, we only have hardy trees and grasses that do not need much water. On the terrace leading from our living room, there are various seats on wooden decking between large stainless steel plant pots with feathery grasses and trees. The lounge sofa and the flowers are in matching colours: red, orange and purple.'

Family and friends, as well as other interested people, are welcome to visit your terrace.

'Our penthouse was the model home that could be visited during the construction period. When we bought it, we were asked if we would like to be part of the Rotterdam Tours' guided tour of the Timmerhuis. I love architecture myself and really enjoy visiting other buildings, so I thought it would be fun to do my part. Since then, we frequently welcome tours on Fridays. Each tour lasts no more than a quarter of an hour. A number of neighbours are part of the tour on other days.'

Do the visitors walk straight through to the rooftop terrace?

'Absolutely. The patio doors are always open and the terrace is so inviting. It is great to hear all the enthusiastic reactions and see the visitors enjoying the view and taking selfies.'

You received so many enthusiastic reactions that you have even set up your own company organising meetings at your house.

'I came up with the idea for Rotterdam Meetings when, through my work, I attended a brainstorming session in someone's home. Our kitchen and enormous wooden kitchen table are perfect for private meetings for eight to ten people, over a healthy lunch. And the view over the city forms an inspiring backdrop for teams in out-of-office business strategy brainstorming sessions, workshops or trainings.'

From your penthouse, you have a good view of the many vacant black rooftops in the city centre.

'Yes. It is such a waste. This is a forgotten part of the city because it can't be seen from the street. So much more could be done with these rooftops. We were really made aware of this when we participated in the Rotterdam Rooftop Days. We hope that the rooftops around us will become greener and livelier over the coming years. The rooftop terraces of the Timmerhuis show how much fun it can be.'

Zen above the clouds

A high rooftop is the perfect place to relax and enjoy the Rotterdam skyline. Arthur Suiker lives in the luxury penthouse of the Montevideo apartment building on the Wilhelminapier, with rooftop terraces on the 42nd and the 43rd floors. 'From the jacuzzi, the window in the parapet looks out over the river Nieuwe Maas towards Pernis. In the evening when everything is lit up, you can imagine you are in Paris: the curves of the Maas are just like those of the Seine.'

—

Who? Arthur Suiker, entrepreneur
Where? Wilhelminapier
On the roof since? 2011
What? 80 m² rooftop terrace on the 42nd floor and 75 m² rooftop terrace on the 43rd floor

Montevideo

Design Montevideo: Mecanoo
Design rooftop terraces: Lennart Otte
Function: wining and dining and private spa
Completion date: 2011
Material: bamboo and mdf (medium density fibreboard)
Access: via the mezzanine on the 42nd floor and through the master bedroom on the 43rd floor

You took advantage of the recession to buy your own Rotterdam penthouse with rooftop terrace.

'Indeed. My philosophy is: save during prosperous times and invest in times of recession. I have worked hard for twenty years, ten of which as an entrepreneur. Six years ago, I was able to buy this apartment for a good price. It was completed in 2006 and had been empty ever since.'

You bought this apartment from Mr. Paarlberg, the real estate trader convicted for money laundering.

'This was one of his investments. You can think what you like about him, but this man has good taste. I have also been to the penthouses in the 100Hoog and the New Orleans apartment complexes, but they are nowhere near as attractive as this apartment. It is so amazingly high. The enormous glass windows allow unobstructed views on all sides. It is the most beautiful place in Rotterdam.'

The penthouse has two rooftop terraces.

'The terrace on the 42nd floor is adjacent to the mezzanine, where my study is located. A computer controlled flower wall surrounds the windows in the parapet, beautifully framing their view of the Rotterdam skyline. I had thought that this terrace would be ideal for wining and dining, but I scarcely ever sit here. I am considering turning it into a green oasis.'

Your favourite terrace is the rooftop terrace on the 43rd floor.

'I had this designed as a Japanese spa. There are wooden split-level platforms and the jacuzzi is continuously heated to 38.5 degrees. There was a basin for a swimming pool, but I had that covered over. If I want to swim, I can do so in the pool on the 3rd floor of this building.'

How do you use this terrace?

'Access is from the master bedroom and the bathroom. In the morning, I go straight from the shower into the jacuzzi. No one can see me. When it isn't windy, it is often surprisingly warm. In the winter, it almost feels like a winter sports holiday. Wrapped in a blanket I thoroughly enjoy the sun.'

This terrace has fewer plants than the terrace below.

'At this height, you have to take the wind into account. There is a sturdy holly bush in a pot. The tree in the middle of the terrace is a Portuguese cork oak. This grows naturally in the mountains of Portugal and can cope with extreme conditions.'

There is one rooftop that is even higher.

'The well-known M, for Montevideo, is located on that rooftop. It is actually a weather vane turning soundlessly in the wind. Do you know the Batman sign? I get that same feeling when I drive into Rotterdam and see the M. The M is my sign. At New Year my partner and I spread a bearskin rug underneath it and enjoy a glass of champagne while watching the fireworks display on the Erasmus Bridge. Did you know that fireworks only rise to about one hundred metres? I was rather disappointed the first time I saw them from here. This roof is 140 metres high.'

I assume many people like to come and visit you.

'I prefer to be alone here. So that I can rest and relax. It is wonderful to take the lift, zooming up at a rate of one floor per second into and sometimes even above the clouds. Everything here is so vast and quiet. The perfect feeling of Zen.'

A rooftop terrace at a stone's throw away from the Hef

The Rotterdam architectural firm Kühne & Co specialises in upgrading cramped, forgotten spaces in the city. This includes finding better uses for rooftops.

Architects Paul Lageschaar and Joost Kühne designed a home for Paul and his partner Jan-Philip van Mourik on a narrow plot of land near the Hef, the fomer railway bridge on the Noordereiland. From their rooftop terrace, 14.5 metres above the ground, they have the 'most beautiful view of Rotterdam. It looks out on the city, the river and the former railway bridge, enchantingly illuminated at night. We sway with the tide and to the rhythm of the ships as they come and go. Proof that the Port of Rotterdam never sleeps.'

Jaffa Poort

Rooftop meetings: a sign of the future (see page 90). This is already happening on the rooftop of the Jaffa Poort apartment block on the Goudse Rijweg in Kralingen. The complex, belonging to Woonstad Housing Corporation, consists of forty subsidised rental apartments designed to 'last a lifetime'. The residents should be able to continue living here until well into their old age. Underneath Jaffa Poort there is a car park, on the rooftop of which the housing corporation commissioned Zoontjens and Binder Groenprojecten to construct an easily accessible community rooftop. The residents can meet each other here, even those who use walking aids.

Woonstad Housing Corporation is investing in the sustainability of all its buildings. Solar panels have been installed on the rooftop of this housing complex.

Oostplein

Since 2017, students have been able to study in comfort on the rooftop of a post-war building near Oostplein. Rien de Groot, together with fellow architect Jasper van Lammeren, designed two furnished penthouses on top of the housing complex on Groenendaal that his father Rinus had built in 1953. The post-war building has been completely renovated.

The luxurious four room rooftop apartments have large glass windows and all have their own 15 m² rooftop terrace. The building inspectors granted permission to build on top of the original building, provided the finished apartments were constructed at least one and a half metres from the edge of the roof. The resulting strip at the edge has become a green roof. Sedum plants and solar panels will be installed on the rooftop of the new apartments.

These rental apartments are intended for wealthier students.

PAUL HEERKENS, ZOONTJENS MANAGING DIRECTOR
TRANSFORMING ROOFTOPS

'Beneficial use of rooftops in cities such as Rotterdam is essential'

For the last eleven years, Tilburg-based Zoontjens has focused on the transformation of unused rooftops, convinced that – with cities becoming more densely populated, warmer and wetter – rooftops are ideally suited for extra usable outdoor space, as well as for cooling and rainwater storage. The company has used its expertise to design and deliver numerous innovative rooftop projects, ranging from landscaped public open spaces to carparks. According to managing director Paul Heerkens: 'For every rooftop there is an opportunity to create a new use'.

Zoontjens has applied these principles to projects throughout the Netherlands and Europe. In Rotterdam, the company constructed the rooftop square on the Erasmus University, the playground rooftop on the Jan Prins School (see page 132), the rooftop terraces on The Timmerhuis (see page 106) and the community rooftop of the housing association's Jaffa Poort building (see page 116). Zoontjens actively promotes the rooftop transformation concept, sharing projects on their website and via social media. 'By showing what is possible, we hope to inspire others to make use of their rooftops.'

Re-thing rooftops

At the turn of the century, Paul saw that other European cities were already developing their rooftops. 'Copenhagen focused on ecological aspects, Hamburg was already creating a second city layer and in Stuttgart all new rooftops were green. And then there was London, where the former mayor introduced planning policies requiring green and usable roofs on developments to make the city greener. So, London rooftops are now being used for residents' and public open space, sport and other uses. 'As the London mayor said: "The most under-used asset is just above our heads" and I completely agree. Rooftops need to be developed to provide outdoor space for the people of the city, as well as for biodiversity, sustainable rainwater drainage to avoid flooding, combatting urban heat build-up from global warming and generating renewable energy.'

Developments

For these dedicated rooftop transformation applications, Zoontjens developed a lightweight polyester-concrete paving system which puts very little load on the roofs.' Zoontjens also developed a fall-arrest system. And the company worked with other specialists in lighting, street furniture, planting and energy generation technology.' 'Bitumen and gravel rooftops are outdated. They radiate heat and do nothing to stop rapid rainwater drain-off flooding our sewers. It is an important challenge to find ways to store water on rooftops and to make use of the sun's energy. At the end of next year, Zoontjens intends to market a new rooftop paving system with integrated rainwater storage.'

Raising Awareness

Architects and project developers in the Netherlands have traditionally used the rooftop to simply keep the weather out, at least cost. But recently Paul is seeing a turn around. 'There was a lack of awareness of other possibilities but now the rooftop is being seen as potential functional space. Rotterdam is setting the trend – and justly so. Zoontjens has invested heavily in this change. For many years now, we have been encouraging architects to consider designing buildings with rooftops at different levels. For example, a works canteen could be arranged with rooftop terrace, thereby enabling the workers to easily get fresh air. Construction costs might be slightly higher but the tangible benefits and return on investment in city property are impressive. Standing on a rooftop is a unique experience – like entering a different world. The more people who experience that special feeling, the more the interest in rooftop transformations will spread.'

'Our goal is to inspire everyone to make use of their rooftops'

A rooftop for the city

During a five-week period in the summer of 2016, more than 368,000 people climbed the temporary stairs to the rooftop of the Groot Handelsgebouw office block. They strolled on the rooftop and enjoyed the view, looked at the photo exhibition and treated themselves to an ice cream or lunch. 'It was the main talking point of the city. The endless stream of people was incredible', recalls Marius Meurs. Normally, the rooftop of the largest shared office building in the Netherlands belongs to its 180 tenants. 'But we are giving parts of it back to the city'.

—

Who? Marius Meurs, managing director of N.V. Vennootschap Groot Handelsgebouw
Where? Stationsplein
On the roof since? 1953
What? Sedum, rooftop terraces, public rooms and The Suicide Club

Groot Handelsgebouw

Design: Maaskant and Van Tijen

Status: national monument

Function: office block

Completion date: 1953

Renovation period: 2002-2005

Architect: architectural firm

J. van Stigt

Material: sedum, gravel

Access: stairs from various

locations in the offices

Temporary Stairs Winy Maas:

May-June 2016

During the 'Rotterdam celebrates the city' festival, the stairs to the roof of the Groot Handelsgebouw office block were such a success that it was even suggested that they should be made permanent.

'There are several reasons why that isn't possible. The stream of visitors was too much for the building. Every day, tens of thousands of people climbed the stairs (see page 127) to reach the rooftop and a further hundred wheelchair users used the lift. Our core business is letting offices. All these visitors inconvenienced our tenants. The designer of the stairs, Winy Maas (see page 138) had sketched an outdoor escalator leading to the roof. However, the Stationsplein is a high-risk area so such a construction was not permissible. Furthermore, the escalator would have to be 45 metres high. I have been on a similar escalator in Hong Kong and I think that many people would not enjoy the experience.'

If you rent office space in the Groot Handelsgebouw, do you always have access to the rooftop?

'Yes. The 7,000 m² rooftop terrace is divided into five separate terraces. Access is via various doors from the uppermost storey. It is a wonderful place to go for a stroll, have a discussion or just sit among the sedum and the green pergolas. Each terrace has a beautiful view of a different part of the city: the harbour, the station and the Weena, one of Rotterdam's main roads, or the district Rotterdam North. In the spring of 2017, on the site of Central Station's former bicycle park, a 2nd floor rooftop terrace was created and furnished with specially designed office furniture. This was an immediate success. You can work there all day, sitting on the benches at the long wooden tables between huge light-blue plant pots. It has become the perfect meeting place. Furthermore, for the last fifteen years, a child day care centre with its own rooftop playground has been located on this floor.'

The courtyard and the rooftops of the Groot Handelsgebouw are much greener than you would expect from the rugged outside facade.

'We think it is very important that a building should be green. And, so do our tenants. The presence of plants and greenery, in stark contrast with the concrete and asphalt of the inner city, is one of the reasons why companies choose to locate here. The higher you rise in the building, the greener it becomes. Plants grow in the courtyard and on the balconies and terraces. The offices on the roof look out onto colourful sedum. This is not only beautiful, but also sustainable. The sedum captures rainwater and provides insulation. For this, we have been awarded the energy classification A-label Excellence BREEAM in-use (Building Research Establishment Environmental Assessment Method).'

> ## 'The Suicide Club is a perfect start to achieving our aim of giving the Groot Handelsgebouw back to the city'
> —

In June 2015, The Suicide Club, the first rooftop bar in Rotterdam, opened on your rooftop. This club is accessible to the general public.

'Joint owner Nikki van Dijk came up with the idea of setting up an exclusive club (see page 152) on the rooftop. We were enthralled. The main problem was: how to reach the club from the street? The only access is via the goods lift that comes out into the kitchen. An enticing gimmick. People would think: where on earth am I? This rooftop is a perfect start to achieving our aims of giving the Groot Handelsgebouw back to the city.'

What more is in store for the general public?

'We intend to restore the Kriterion to its former function of cinema, theatre and conference centre. We will renovate this 1950s hall and intend to find a professional party to manage the programming. A particular point that needs to be addressed is its accessibility for those who are less mobile. You can take the lift to the foyer on the 7th floor but from there, the only access up to the 8th floor is by stairs. Furthermore, we would like to dismantle the Kriterion's rooftop lounge Under the Stars. It is in such bad condition that renovation is not possible. But, we don't intend to demolish anything until we have guarantees about what will replace it. After all, everyone is aware that this rooftop has so much potential. You never know what new possibilities the future will bring.'

ROOFTOP GROOT HANDELSGEBOUW WITH THE SUICIDE CLUB

Temporary stairs to the Groot Handelsgebouw

During a five-week period in the summer of 2016, more than 368,000 people climbed the temporary stairs to the rooftop of the Groot Handelsgebouw office block. They strolled on the rooftop and enjoyed the view, looked at the photo exhibition and treated themselves to an ice cream or lunch. It was the main talking point of the city. The scaffolding stairs were designed by Rotterdam firm of architects MVRDV – renowned for the Markthal – for Rotterdam celebrates the city, an event celebrating 75 years of post-war reconstruction. On page 138, Winy Maas, the figurehead for MVRDV, argues for the speedy development of Rotterdam's rooftops'.

Van Oord

Design: De Jong Gortemaker
Developer: OVG Project
Developers
Commissioned by: Van Oord
Contractor: Dura Vermeer
Material: concrete/steel
Access: via folding glass doors
Construction period: ABC-wing
2009-2012; D-wing 2012-2015
**ABC-wing sedum rooftop,
constructed by:** Van Rosmalen
**D-wing green rooftop,
constructed by:** Binder
Groenprojecten

An ode to the fifth facade

Maritime contractor Van Oord went to a lot of effort to design the rooftops of the new head office at the foot of the Van Brienenoord Bridge. The building, the Nieuwe Maas, has 4,800 m² of sedum rooftops and 3,000 m² of hardwood rooftop terrace. 'We decided to make the rooftops beautiful for the benefit of motorists driving over the Van Brienenoord Bridge: to give them a lovely view.'

—

Who? Erik Visser, building manager
Where? Schaardijk
On the roof since? 2009
What? Sedum and hardwood terraces

You have even hidden the antennae.

'It doesn't matter how beautiful the rest of a building is, if the rooftop is dotted with cooling installations and antennae it will still look ugly. In our building, the technical installations are in the cellar and the rooftop is neat and tidy. The sedum rooftops are delightful to look at, especially in summer. The tall plumes sway elegantly in the wind.'

Did the construction of the sedum rooftops lead to any problems?

'When sedum is saturated with rainwater it becomes extremely heavy. The roof needs to be able to cope with this. As we learnt by trial and error. There was considerable leakage in the ABC-wing. This was partly due to inexperience and partly due to time constraints around the official opening by the then Crown Prince Willem-Alexander. This problem was eventually solved, but only after substantial renovation of the new building, involving the complete replacement of the bitumen sealing under the sedum layer.'

That didn't deter you.

'We learnt a lot during the first phase of construction. For the D-wing, that was added later, the construction company Dura Vermeer hired in expertise from Binder Groenprojecten. That was a good move. Not a single leak. I would choose sedum rooftops any time, provided there is expert supervision.'

Are the terraces for employees only?

'Employees can make use of the inner garden on the rooftop of the car park and the terrace belonging to the company canteen. During lunchtime, on sunny days, it is completely full. Higher up, there are three rooftop terraces each leading out from a different room. One terrace belongs to the Van Oordzaal, the boardroom in which important contracts are regularly signed. Another belongs to the large meeting room and the third terrace is next to our Van Oord museum, the House of Heritage. An outdoor exhibition of large nautical objects may soon be set up on the museum rooftop terrace. Motorists will also be able to see this'.

Have you considered rainwater collection?

'Yes. The rainwater flows from the roofs via drainage pipes directly into the river Nieuwe Maas, thereby relieving the sewers. After a heavy shower the water gushes under our water taxi jetty and into the river.'

What maintenance do the rooftops require?

'Right now, five years on, everything is running smoothly. The sedum rooftops require regular maintenance and the hardwood terraces need to be scrubbed clean each year. There is plenty for a manager to do here.'

What is it like being manager of a building like this?

'It's a great privilege. This building is my second home. I have been involved with it from its conception in 2009. It is a vast building: 22,000 m² for eight hundred employees. And it is sustainable: nearly all the materials can be completely recycled and we have an installation for heat and cold storage.'

Jan Prins and Willibrord Schools

Design: Arconiko Architects
Commissioned by: Jeugd Onderwijs en Samenleving Rotterdam (Youth Services Rotterdam)
Existing building: former Social Academy, dating from the nineteen seventies
Material: concrete surrounded by an iron fence
Roofing company: Zoontjens
Access: a stairway
Construction period: 2007-2008
Contractor: J.P. van Eesteren

A cool rooftop playground

As more and more families move into the city and new building construction takes away play space on the streets, one option is to consider going upwards. Pupils from the Jan Prins Montessori Junior School and the Willibrord Catholic Primary School have been running and climbing on the school rooftop playground for years now. Dangerous? Not at all.

—

Who? Willemijn Kuijper, headmistress of the Jan Prins School;
10-11 year's old Djaliviah, Leah, Elin, Genesis, Moon-Elin and Mariëly
Where? Nieuwstraat
On the roof since? 2009
What? School playground

Willemijn Kuijper, headmistress Jan Prins School

Why a school playground on the rooftop?
'We had no choice. Our previous school building had to make way for the Markthal, so we moved into the building next door. There is a school playground at street level, but it is not big enough. The original idea was to construct a playing area in the inner courtyard, but the neighbours put a stop to that. So, we were forced to consider the rooftop. The long part, where the children now play football, was already there. The shorter section was lower than it is now. During the renovation, an extra storey was added.'

Are parents worried when they realise that the school playground is 14 metres above the ground?
'No. They love the school playground. And there is no need to worry: the railings are safe enough to meet even the toughest of safety standards.'

Is the rooftop used often?
'Children play in the playground from early morning until late in the evening, depending on the weather and the daylight. The school has 700 pupils, the youngest 200 of whom play on the playground below. During breaks, three classes, up to 75 children, play on the roof at any one time. All pupils stay at school for lunch and some stay for after school care. The clock on the Laurenskerk allows everyone to keep track of break time.'

Does the school playground meet all your requirements?
'We would prefer to see more plants and nature. Natural science, care for the environment and playing in natural environments are core aspects of Montessori education. Together with the Willibrord School, we are trying to find ways to make the rooftop greener, but our two schools have very different ideas. Our first step will be to make the playground at street level much greener.'

What is the playground like when it rains or is very hot?
'There are never any puddles on the rooftop. The tiles are raised so that rainwater trickles through the grooves to the space underneath. When the sun is very hot, we stretch sheets of cloth between posts to create shade. If necessary, we sprinkle water for cooling.'

Pupils
Djaliviah, Leah, Elin, Genesis, Moon-Elin and Mariëly

Are you ever scared of heights?

'No, never. We have been playing here for years and are used to it!'

'One time, I was a bit scared when I climbed up the climbing frame and then had to get back down again. But never when walking along by the railings'

How long have you been playing on this rooftop?

'Since we were 4. When we were younger, our first break was down below and the second up here. During the first break we would look up and shout "aaah". We wanted to be up on the roof. The coolest people were there, and we wanted to be with them.'

Did the playground look like this?

'No. The former rooftop was much greener. There were pots with plants and trees and benches and even some bees. Really beautiful. But the roof started leaking. Then a crane that was building the Market Hall came and took everything away in one go.'

That's a shame.

'Yes, a great shame. But it does mean that we have more room to do fun things. Football, running and table tennis. Now that we are older, we dance and talk a lot. More plants would be nice.'

That net around the football pitch is a good idea.

'Yes, it is, isn't it? Sometimes a ball gets stuck and someone has to climb to get it. That is exciting. A few days ago, a boy threw his shoe up and it stayed hanging in the net. Then it seems very high.'

Do you enjoy being able to see the ceiling of the Markthal?

'That's fun. In winter, and especially at Christmas, it is beautiful. We saw the Markthal being built. In the beginning, we were sometimes angry about all the noise. The bonk, bonk of the piles. 2,400 of them!'

135

JOEP KLABBERS, INITIATOR AND ORGANISER
THE ROTTERDAM ROOFTOP DAYS

'Rotterdam is most unattractive when viewed from high-rise buildings'

During the annual Rotterdam Rooftop Days, it becomes blatantly apparent how ugly Rotterdam's rooftops are. 'Rotterdam is becoming a city of high-rise buildings. From the street, it looks fantastic. But from up high, it is a completely different story. The ugly fifth facades are in urgent need of improvement.'

Architect Joep Klabbers is the initiator and, together with designer and moderator Léon van Geest, organizer of the Rotterdam Rooftop Days. In 2017, the 3rd edition of this festival enticed 10,000 people onto the rooftops of Rotterdam. 'That's the limit. For the 4th edition we are concentrating on quality rather than quantity. The main emphasis of this festival is not to show everyone all these wonderful places, but to ensure that rooftops become an integral part of the city.'

Potential

In 2015, the aim of the 1st edition of the Rotterdam Rooftop Days was to demonstrate the potential of the 1 km² of wasted rooftops in the centre of Rotterdam. Joep: 'That's the equivalent of 150 football fields of neglected building land. It is strange that nothing is being done with it.'

The festival demonstrated to building owners, urban planners and the general public that rooftops can become an extension of public space. The 1st edition attracted thousands of residents and tourists to the rooftops and won the International Festivals & Events Association's Gold Pinnacle Award for Best Small Event.

High-rise city

A year later, the 2nd edition coincided with the post-war reconstruction festival 'Rotterdam celebrates the city', with the top attraction being the temporary stairs designed by architectural firm MVRDV (see page 126 and 138), leading to the roof of the Groot Handelsgebouw (see page 122). 'The stairs attracted people from far and wide to Rotterdam and to the rooftops.'

The next step was to professionalise the festival. The 3rd edition's programming included public rooftops, custom tours and specials. 'Living on Rooftops' was the theme of the seminars and workshops for professionals on the Friday preceding the festival weekend. Participants were shown examples, devised by studio Licht Verdicht (see pages 84 and 92), of new buildings that could be built on top of existing buildings. 'That project led to innovative ideas that we hope will be implemented.'

> **'This festival is our contribution to creating an attractive, sustainable, healthy, resilient city'**
>
> ─

Integral

Evaluation of the 3rd edition led to the suggestion that the focus for the next festival should be on the integral development of rooftops. 'Léon and I are most interested in living, working and relaxing on rooftops. However, compacting – creating additional living space in the city centre – alone is not sufficient. Sustainability, health, energy transition and climate adaptation issues must also be tackled if the city is to become resilient and ready for the future.'

Agenda

The Rotterdam Rooftop Days were never intended to be just another architectural festival. 'Let us be clear about this: we are not here to simply organise a festival. The Rotterdam Rooftop Days are our contribution to creating an attractive, sustainable, futureproof, healthy, resilient city. We will continue to organise this festival for as long as is necessary. Our hope is that it will eventually become redundant, that this festival will seem rather silly when rooftops are accessible all over the city. Unfortunately, we do not expect this to be the case within the next five years.'

NY MAAS, ARCHITECT
FFERENT PERSPECTIVE FROM THE ROOFTOPS

'A refreshingly different perspective from the rooftops'

Rotterdam architectural firm MVRDV is a pioneer in the use of rooftops. Well known rooftop projects in the city include the striking blue Didden Village and last year's temporary stairs to the roof of the Groot Handelsgebouw. If it were up to figurehead Winy Maas, the city will speed up development of its rooftops. 'Rotterdam has the perfect foundation. Make use of it, I say'

Winy's ideal rooftop is green. 'No, not sedum green, but woods and parks. Rooftops should be returned to nature. Preferably I would like to give the whole of Rotterdam a green "Magnum Dip", a layer of nature over the rooftops.'

Potential obstacles are shrugged aside. 'What do you mean, too much wind up there? The rooftop park on the Depot (see page 200) will simply be surrounded by high, glass walls. And a heavy layer of soil? So what? Construction designs can be adjusted.'

Compensation

MVRDV designed the Depot for the Boijmans van Beuningen Museum to give the general public access to the museum depot's art treasures. Over the coming years, the cylinder-shaped building will slowly rise out of the Museum Park, mirroring the surrounding green. The rooftop will become a public park. 'The design of the facade and the rooftop park are intended to compensate for the nature that has had to be sacrificed on the ground. Without these elements, the Depot would be like a fat, introverted gentleman with little to say. We want everyone to enjoy this welcoming building and its environment'. From 2019, the rooftop park will be accessible via a lift in the central hall of the building.

Stairs

Winy would like to make many more rooftops in the city accessible. His vision, The Next Steps, includes outdoor stairs leading from the streets to the rooftops of the Bijenkorf, the Doelen and the Kunsthal, with bridges between the rooftops. He presented this vision last year at the Rotterdam Rooftop Days (see page 136 and 140), the festival of which he is supervisory board member and patron saint. 'It is a brilliant event showing the city from a different, refreshing perspective. A perspective that should be available more often: the uncluttered, panoramic views are so inspiring. It makes people proud of the city. And you see them thinking that they could do this with their own rooftop.'

Legislation

MVRDV looks to Paris and other cities for inspiration. Winy is a consultant for the Grand Paris urban plan, intended to launch the French capital further into the 21st century. 'New legislation entitles everyone in the city to add an extra storey to their building, provided that solar panels are installed on the rooftop. And no, that does not have to be ugly. Technicians in South Korea have developed solar cells on rods. These can be as tall as four metres high.

Placed above the ventilation installation, this creates a pergola over the rooftop terrace. This would be a great idea in Rotterdam. If it were up to me, we would really set to work on this.'

Cool

MVRDV's latest rooftop design involves a village of fifty homes on a large rooftop in Rotterdam city centre. 'With a real wood people can wander through.' This is all that Winy is able to tell us about it because the investor has not yet committed. 'The construction with all its stairs is not cheap. I really hope it goes ahead. It is a really cool plan.'

'No, not sedum green, but woods and parks on the rooftops'

Westblaak Carpark on the Thornico Building

Each year, Westblaak Carpark on the Thornico Building (at the bottom of the photo) is the main location for the Rotterdam Rooftop Days. This rooftop is twenty metres above the ground and has a beautiful view of the skyline of Rotterdam. The visitors on the right are standing on the highest rooftop of the building. At 45 metres above the ground, this rooftop is home to highest colonies of bees in the city. The three colonies, each in their own hive, add to the city centre's natural resources and produce more than 100 kg of honey each year.

During the summer period, the Westblaak Carpark (see page 6) also forms the décor for DÂK with festivities, live music, local DJs and a 'social barbecue'.

On top of a post-war reconstruction icon

The main obstacle to opening the rooftop of the 5th floor of the Bijenkorf (department store) to the general public is its inaccessibility. It can only be reached via the office floors. In spite of this, the Bijenkorf organises more and more events on the rooftop. 'We want to explicitly join in with events in the city and exploitation of our unique post-war reconstruction rooftop is a perfect opportunity.'

—

Who? Lot Defoort, Events Manager
Where? Coolsingel
On the roof since? 2013
What? Events

Bijenkorf

Design: Marcel Breuer and Abraham Elzas

Commissioned by: the Bijenkorf's management

Size of the 5th floor rooftop: about 3,500 m²

Access: stairs from the offices

Material: gravel

Construction period: 1953-1957

It would never have occurred to the architect of this historic building that people would enjoy going onto the rooftop.

'No, it was never Marcel Breuer's intention that the rooftop would be a place to do anything. That is why the visitors' lift only goes as far as the 3rd floor, the highest shopping floor. When an event is held on the roof, the visitors report to the 3rd floor kitchen department and we then escort them through the offices to the stairs leading to the rooftop. It is not possible to extend the lift as far as the 5th floor, so a permanent rooftop café is not currently feasible.'

He did however pay particular attention to the design of the rooftops on the 4th floor.

'There are three patios. Breuer constructed these to provide enough daylight for the employees in the offices. When the weather permits, we lunch at the picnic tables on the middle patio. Recently bee hotels have been installed on the other two patios. Solitary wild bees lay their eggs in the hotels and the bees that hatch can hibernate there. Our aim is to grow plants and flowers on the 5th floor rooftop to provide food for the bees on the patio and from surrounding areas.'

The 5th floor rooftop offers a unique view of the city centre

'We are proud of our building, a post-war reconstruction icon. From the rooftop, you can clearly see that this building has been here longer than any other. The surrounding buildings are newer and higher. The green colouring of many of the surrounding rooftops is particularly noticeable, for example the World Trade Centre and the Town Hall Tower.'

The Bijenkorf organises more and more events on this rooftop.

'Last year was the fourth year in succession that performances were given on our rooftop as part of the Rotterdam Opera Days. Tickets were sold out within thirty minutes. For the occasion, we set up a tent to partially cover the rooftop. Last year we also organised a Rooftop Festival for our Bijenkorf members. Activities took place throughout the whole day: breakfast, yoga, sport, lunch, grill, drinks and a party. The Cape Verdean Sodade Festival, in the Doelen (concert hall), provided another opportunity to party on the rooftop.'

The rooftop was completely transformed for the Rotterdam Rooftop Days in June 2017.

'Together with the festival organisers (see page 136), we created a sculpture garden with statues that had been on the Coolsingel in front of the temporary shops during the post-war reconstruction years. On Saturdays and Sundays in June, as well as during the Rooftop Days themselves, visitors could enjoy the exposition, walking around the rooftop on a footpath through the gravel. A pop-up terrace provided coffee and excellent views. It was a huge success.'

OPERA DAYS ON THE BIJENKORF

Hofbogen

Design rooftop Hofplein Station: ZUS designers

Status: national monument

Length: 1.9 kilometres; the longest rooftop in the Netherlands

Size: 5,500 m²

Function: under the arches: cafés, restaurants and creative entrepreneurs in the fields of fashion, food, design and health; on the rooftop: parks, plants and events

Completion date: 2015

Material: grass, botanical garden, orchard, covered concrete platform

Access: via the former station stairs and via the Luchtsingel (wooden airbridge)

146

Everyone's rooftop

Who? Addy van der Knaap, Managing Director Hofbogen B.V.
Where? The roof of Hofplein Station
On the roof since? 2015
What? Rooftop park, a covered platform, orchard, botanical garden, a playground bank under construction, events area

147

With its 1.9 kilometres, Hofbogen is the longest rooftop in the Netherlands. The rooftop of Hofplein Station is a popular location for events. If no event is taking place, the events area of the rooftop is closed. Next year, the aim is to permanently open this part of the rooftop to the general public. There are many plans for the rest of the roof, but no decisions have yet been taken.

Who owns the Hofbogen?

'The Hofbogen railway arches belong to the Havensteder and Vestia housing corporations. In 2006, they jointly set up Hofbogen B.V. to purchase this neglected viaduct in order to restore it to its former glory and so actively contribute to improving the neighbourhood.'

Who owns the Hofbogen rooftop?

'A better question would be: who doesn't? Everyone seems to think they own the rooftop: the entrepreneurs under the railway arches, the city council, the district committee, the volunteers who work together with Binder Groenprojecten to look after the plants and local residents as well as other people of Rotterdam. Officially, the roof of the Hofplein Station belongs to Hofbogen B.V., as does the roof of the Bergweg Station. The rest of the

famiri

148

'Who owns the
Hofbogen rooftop?
A better question
would be: who
doesn't?'

STATION
HOFPLEIN

kijk me ogen, luister me oren

149

rooftop currently belongs to ProRail, who are responsible for railway infrastructure. However, since 2010, trains no longer travel over the Hofbogen, so ProRail would like to sell their share. If it is sold, Rotterdam City Council will be awarded the building and planting rights. Given the current situation involving three parties, decision making becomes extremely complicated.'

Hofbogen B.V. have restored the Hofbogen railway arches.

'This national monument had fallen into decay. We are restoring it, in phases, using our own funds together with contributions from the EU's European Regional Development Fund. ZUS's design for the section of rooftop over the Hofplein Station is an extension of the Luchtsingel. It includes an events podium, fifty seats each shaped like a sheep, a botanical garden and an orchard. The rooftop park is not yet fully completed. We still need to restore the railway platform – the concrete is very uneven – and construct a plastic playground bank at the edge of the events area. This will be a place where children play and parents relax. The L-shaped playground bank is in keeping with the theme that ZUS

devised for the rooftop: a glimpse of the polder landscape through which trains once travelled.'

You were also responsible for the programming for the roof.

'We have just completed a busy festival season, including the *silent rooftop cinema* Roffa mon Amour, the RYPP wine festival, the Rotterdam Opera Days, yoga evenings, the Rotterdam Rooftop Days (see pages 136 and 140) and Hofplein Theatre Group children's shows. By doing this, we hope to make the Hofbogen hip and attractive to a varied public and to demonstrate the potential of the rooftop. However, we are not an events agency. We do not have the facilities for this.'

What do the neighbours think about these events on the rooftop?

'Generally, they join in and enjoy them. There are of course occasional complaints about the noise. We are currently meeting with the neighbouring residents to discuss a framework within which rooftop events are acceptable. Keeping on good terms with the neighbourhood is very important and we hope to improve the quality of life in the area.'

What happens when no festival is taking place on the rooftop?

'Nothing, I am sorry to say. The area is closed off. We would love the rooftop to be accessible to everyone and we are actually making preparations so that this will be possible after the Rotterdam Rooftop Days in June 2018.'

Will everyone be able to go onto the rooftop night and day?

'There will probably be designated opening times; the gate will open and close at specific times. We hope to find a restaurant or café owner who would like to set up business on the roof and who would also be responsible for the management and the organisation of events. Various parties have already shown interest.'

Hofbogen B.V. hopes to sell the Hofbogen.

'Yes. Vestia and Havensteder are housing corporations and need to focus on their core business: public housing. Autonomous, professional real estate is not part of that.'

What will it cost?

'I can't tell you exactly. But given the high costs of the initial acquisition and the investments we have already made for the

restoration, we are aiming for the highest possible proceeds.'

Is interest being shown?

'Yes. In recent years, various parties have shown interest. We are currently preparing a tender with a transparent process. We expect it to take another year and a half before the Hofbogen are actually sold.'

What does the future hold for the longest rooftop in the Netherlands?

'That is not yet clear. Everyone has ideas (see pages 186 and 198). The city council would like to turn it into a public park with a continuous walking route from the rooftop of the Hofplein Station up to, and maybe even over, the A20 motorway. Café and restaurant owners in the arches would love to have rooftop terraces. Happy Italy in Bergweg Station hopes to open a terrace in 2018. Architects have presented sketches of houses above the rooftop with the park meandering underneath. Local residents would like to have an own garden there and, in addition, there is also a plan to convert the rooftop into an aqua duct. As has already been mentioned, the roof belongs to everyone. Decision making becomes very complicated.'

ROFFA MON AMOUR

The Suicide Club

—

Design: Mehdi le Mair

Commissioned by: Mess

Size: 200 m² indoors and 500 m² outdoors

Access: a goods lift that comes out into the kitchen

Former function: the former events room belonging to bar & restaurant Engels

Material: interior: brass, singed wood, turquoise paintwork, oak parquet, bare steel

Renovation: 2015

152

Something risqué on the rooftop

In 2015, The Suicide Club on the rooftop of the Groot Handelsgebouw became Rotterdam's first rooftop bar. Mess, the devisers and owners of the Biergarten bar and restaurant Ayla, came up with the idea of setting up a club on this historic rooftop. 'We wanted to create an edgy grunge style international club, at the limits of your comfort zone.'

—

Who? Nikki van Dijk, joint owner
Where? Stationsplein
On the roof since? 2015
What? Rooftop bar

Why does hip and happening Rotterdam have only one rooftop bar?

'No idea! After the opening of The Suicide Club, we expected others to quickly follow. But, since then, nothing has happened. Even though there really is demand for rooftop bars, like the clubs in Paris, Istanbul and Singapore.'

At the time, the name The Suicide Club was very controversial.

'Everything we do here pushes the limits: the name, the extravagant interior, the flavours of the food, the employees' Rotterdam overalls. The Groot Handelsgebouw (see page 122) wanted something risqué on the rooftop to link the building in with the hip and happening allure of the city. We were inspired by the exciting, steamy clubs of American prohibition: speakeasy secret bars where you needed a password to enter.'

You weren't deterred by the fact that the only way of entering is by using a goods lift.

'On the contrary. Simply getting to the club is a unique experience: through the entrance hall of the Groot Handelsgebouw, searching the courtyard for the entrance to the lift and then the ancient lift itself. As visitor, you feel amazement at being in this special place, being part of this hidden urban jewel.

Then, next surprise, when the lift comes out into the kitchen. You, the visitor, have been admitted via the back door of the club. Is there no end to this sensory experience? And someone will always be there to welcome you: after all, the chefs are in the kitchen preparing food. You feel at home immediately.'

What kind of people come to this club?

'People who appreciate the humour of this concept and enjoy letting their hair down. Innovative people from the Groot Handelsgebouw, expats and an international clientele of cosmopolitans who like to party as they are used to doing in their own country. And local residents who in the past always had to go to Amsterdam for an opportunity to dress up and enjoy the night life in style.'

The Suicide Club has a 500 m² rooftop terrace.

'Yes, it is long and narrow. As it gets busier, we use more and more of the terrace, like an accordion. We have made extra outdoor bars at the beginning and end, where you look out over the station. When the weather is really beautiful, and the place becomes crowded, we open the bar at that end. But that only happens a few times each year.'

You actually only use a very small part of the Groot Handelsgebouw rooftop. Do you have ideas and plans for the rest of the rooftop?

'We've plenty of ideas. Unfortunately, we are much too busy with the club, Biergarten bar and restaurant Ayla to be able to carry them out ourselves. During initial discussions with the owners of the Groot Handelsgebouw, we fantasised about a city park with a jogging route. A functional park for everybody, right next to Central Station, at the heart of the city centre. That is my ultimate dream. But, someone else will have to do it. Just sorting out the permits and licences for this national monument will take at least two years.'

'As it gets busier, we use more and more of the rooftop terrace, like an accordion'

—

BEST ROOFTOP
IN THE NETHERLANDS
2017

The beating heart

Who? Valerie Kuster, creator and manager of Op Het Dak (On The Rooftop)

Where? Schiekade

On the roof since? 2013

What? Organic restaurant on the Schieblock

—

European urban rooftop farms are only profitable in combination with a café or restaurant. Back in 2012, when the DakAkker rooftop farm was constructed on the Schieblock, nobody yet knew this. Food creator Valerie Kuster set up her restaurant in the rooftop pavilion with the aim of getting the neighbourhood involved with the DakAkker. 'This was at the heart of this city initiative. And a heart needs to keep beating and be kept warm, otherwise it will stop.'

At the time, you were squatting in the rooftop pavilion.

'We occupied both the Schieblock and this little house. Traditionally, squatters raise the pirate flag, the Jolly Roger. Ours depicted a skull and carrot – a humorous reference to the vegetable garden. By now the flag is worn and tattered, but that just adds to its charm.'

How did you end up here?

'After eight years of working in London and a year spent travelling, I set up office in the Schieblock. My neighbours were design agency ZUS and the Rotterdams Milieucentrum (RMC, Rotterdam Environment Centre). They had devised and built the DakAkker (see page 74), the Luchtsingel wooden airbridge and the Hofbogen rooftop park (see pages 146, 186 and 198). When I went to take a look at the DakAkker, I spotted this little house. The RMC used it to store their tools and had installed a basic kitchen for use as a canteen. The idea of using this to showcase the project took form. I started a pop-up rooftop café with cooking workshops and

Op Het Dak

Design: Valerie Kuster
Size: 50 m² restaurant, 24 m² terrace
Access: stairs from the Schieblock
Existing building: Schieblock
Function: rooftop pavilion
Renovation: 2012
Manager: Valerie Kuster
Subsidy: Job Dura Fund for the fantastic peepholes

'Every day we serve fresh, enticing, colourful dishes with produce from our own garden'

—

Wednesday lunches. Since then, I have gradually renovated the building.'

How did you engage with the neighbourhood?

'The DakAkker continually yields fresh vegetables and edible flowers. There are many restaurants in the neighbourhood. These two facts are the perfect combination. My company Food Rhapsody had recently organised the Food Festival and I was able to use my network within the Rotterdam food industry to contact chefs in the neighbourhood: Marnix – then from the Biergarten, Jim de Jong, DJ from Kino and Guido from Lokaal. That worked: they bought our harvest and together we organised events whereby a chef prepared a pop-up dinner.'

And so, the heart started beating.

'Indeed. I also put a lot of effort into PR. I published a weekly Facebook blog. And every week I hung up Wednesday lunch menu posters in the Schieblock and businesses in the area. After seeing this five or so times, people start thinking they should try it out. By now, I have built up a regular clientele.'

The pop-up café has grown into a fully fledged restaurant.

'After one hundred Wednesday lunches, I changed tack. On the 1st of March 2016, together with a partner, I founded the rooftop restaurant Op Het Dak. We have a catering and liquor license and can cater for up to 45 people. The DakAkker is a test site, so it continues to produce varying unusual vegetables and fruit. And an ever increasing selection of edible flowers. This means that every day we serve fresh, enticing, colourful dishes with produce from our own garden.'

Are you still trying to engage more with the city?

'Our links are spreading ever further. We buy coffee from Stielman and beer from local brewers Brouwerij Noord and the Kaapse Brouwers. And much of our PR takes place through Rotterdam food bloggers and Rotterdam Partners, the city's (inter)national PR office. Tourists easily find us. The DakAkker also participates in the Rotterdam Rooftop Days in June each year (see page 140), we organise our own events and the city council regularly brings international delegations to visit the place. Of course, there are still some people – even in Rotterdam – who do not know that Op Het Dak exists, but that is not really a problem. I know for sure that we have made our mark.'

Stroom

Design: Robert Winkel Architects, Mei architects and planners
Status: national monument.
Existing building: Stroom is located in the former transformer house in the Schiecentrale, the electricity station that provided electricity for the port of Rotterdam until the 1990s
Size: 170 m²
Function: rooftop for hosting events
Completion date: 2005
Material: concrete tiles and plants
Access: by lift or stairs via the topmost storey of the hotel

A flexible rooftop

Who? Jantiene Berg, together with Edwin van der Meijde,
owner-managers of hotel-brasserie Stroom
Where? Lloydstraat
On the roof since? 2013
What? Weddings and parties, rooftop parties, barbecues,
yoga and a mini film house festival

—

Keeping the neighbours happy is the biggest challenge when exploiting a rooftop terrace. The owners of the Stroom hotel-brasserie rooftop terrace are well aware of this. 'We have made great efforts to earn the good will of our neighbours. And we expect a certain level of tolerance in return. After all, living in a city, you have to accept a certain amount of noise.'

How do you use the rooftop terrace?
'Our hotel guests drink coffee on the rooftop in the morning or relax there with a sundowner after a day in the city. During the summer, we give Sunday morning yoga lessons. This is a longstanding dream come true for me and for the neighbourhood. Every week during the wedding season – May / June and August / September – couples come to the rooftop to say: "I do."

Business barbecues also regularly take place. In January and June, we organise our own Rooftop parties and last September we held our first silent mini film house festival, programmed by the Roffa mon Amour (see page 146). Over the years, my deeply rooted dreams for our rooftop terrace are slowly coming true.'

Your rooftop terrace is forever changing
'We change the furnishings of the rooftop terrace depending on the activity. The only permanent elements are the three fig trees in plant pots. They were already here when we took over the place and they weigh two thousand kilos each, so we can't just shift them around. This year my brother designed tables to go around them, with space for people to sit. They look really good. The rest is completely flexible: the outdoor bar is on wheels and this summer we replaced

the heavy benches, that were already here, with functional furniture that is much easier to move.'

Is it possible to dine on the rooftop?

'We organise this about fourteen times each year. The brasserie furniture is carried up to the rooftop to create a pop-up restaurant. But we do need to be sure that it is going to stay warm. The high Schiecentrale behind us blocks the sun and the wind frequently blows from the sea. This does not necessarily make it too cold on the rooftop, but experience has shown that at temperatures of 21 degrees or cooler, people ask if they can go inside once they have had their starter. On cooler evenings, we recommend that our guests enjoy their aperitif on the rooftop but go indoors to eat. And yes, this does sometimes require all our powers of persuasion.'

Do people come to Stroom especially for the rooftop terrace?

'The rooftop terrace definitely gives the building a kind of sexiness, certainly now there is much more focus on rooftops. But a rooftop terrace alone is not sufficient to make your place a popular hangout. You need to provide the total package. We do this by making the neighbourhood more attractive with our brasserie and the bakers shop where fresh bread is baked daily.'

What about noise disturbing the neighbours?

'If there is too much noise, then that is because the people on the rooftop make sounds. Even at silent discos you can hear people singing along. You also hear the general background buzz and bridal couples saying "I do" into the microphone. Residents in the Schiecentrale do of course notice the noise very quickly. But sometimes we receive complaints from someone living three hundred metres away. We need to be very careful because noise can carry a long way.'

'The rooftop terrace definitely gives the building a kind of sexiness'

—

How do you do that? Be careful about the noise?

'Right from the start, we invested in good relations with the neighbourhood. When we organise our Rooftop Party, I send letters to all the home owners' associations inviting the neighbours to come early at 19:00 for a personal welcome drink and explanation.

Frequently, only about ten residents make use of this invitation, but those that come greatly appreciate it. I think it is important to explain what we do. By being totally honest and open, I aim to cultivate understanding. And it seems to be working.'

Are there special regulations for the exploitation of a rooftop terrace?

'No different than for any other catering establishment. We need to keep noise levels below the maximum permissible number of decibels and adhere to regulation closing times. We need to be quiet from 23:00, which means we start tidying up at 22:00. For at most five times a year, we can apply for a permit to stay open until 02:00. Since we have been here, we have always done that for our Winter Rooftop Party in the second week of January and for our Summer Rooftop Party in the middle of June. The winter party in particular is fantastic. Last time, we welcomed 350 guests, many of them young parents from the neighbourhood who had arranged baby sitters and had come to meet each other. There were also eight DJs and a pig on a spit. The wind chill temperature during the winter edition is on average -8 degrees, so everyone wears thick jackets and woolly hats. In the summer, we have an outdoor cocktail bar serving gin and tonics and a barbecue.'

What do the hotel guests think about the activities on the rooftop?

'Frequently, they join in themselves, either because that is the reason for their visit or because they take part in for example the yoga lessons. We always take our guests into account, as eleven of the 21 hotel rooms look out onto the rooftop terrace. Activities on the rooftop begin at 10:00 at the earliest and end at 22:00, so that we still have an hour in which to clear everything away. Anyone out late dining or partying in the city or on our rooftop has plenty of opportunity to sleep in the next morning. After 23:00 all is quiet.'

What was your best moment on the rooftop terrace last year?

'That was a summer evening during the weekend of the Port of Rotterdam North Sea Jazz Festival. When I came up onto the rooftop, people were cosily leaning against each other on the benches. Beneath the starry sky, savouring the glow of a wonderful day of music, gazing at the beautiful Rotterdam skyline. It was so serene and romantic. The best compliment our rooftop terrace could ever receive.'

STROOM WINTER ROOFTOP PARTY

Bistro

Binnenrotte

Bistro Binnenrotte's first floor terrace is known as the "Stadsterras" - City Terrace. 'City Rooftop Terrace' would work just as well as the terrace is situated on the rooftop of the Central Library's entrance hall. From the terrace, there are magnificent views of the Markthal, Blaak Station, the Cube Houses and the Laurenskerk. From the end of 2018, you will also be able to follow the construction of Rotta Nova, the new residential complex to be built on the grass strip between the Markthal and the Hoofdstraat.

Access to the rooftop terrace is via the Bistro Bar on the ground floor and via the 1st floor of the Central Library. The Bistro Bar is open seven days a week for lunch, drinks and dinner. The rooftop terrace is open whenever the weather permits. On market days, you look out over the awnings of the stalls on the Binnenrotte.

Pakhuismeesteren

Design: AWG Architects

Commissioned by: VolkerWessels concern, Van Agtmaal BV contractors

Existing building: The warehouses Celebes, Borneo, Java and Sumatra belonging to the former Pakhuismeesteren company, municipal monument (foundations date from 1898; reconstruction 1941)

Rooftop function: 3500 m² of hotel rooms, conference halls and terraces on the 3rd and 4th floor; a joint rooftop terrace with outdoor bar on the 5th floor

Exploitation: lifestyle hotel run by the Spanish hotel chain Room Mate Hotels

Physical Construction: completely new foundations under the building and a new lower level cellar floor for the car park

Material: hard wood, zinc, glass and epdm (ethylene propylene diene monomer) roofing

Access: two new lift shafts, two new stairwells and two existing emergency stairways

Construction period: 2015-2017

Owner and developer: Van Agtmaal BV contractors

On historic foundations

Pakhuismeesteren on the Wilhelminapier is a classic example of new construction on an old building. This completely renovated historic warehouse has been transformed into a lifestyle hotel with two new hotel storeys and rooftop terraces. Van Agtmaal Contractors was responsible for the construction and the quirky design of this hotel, which opened last autumn. 'We like to take our clients here to demonstrate what is possible on a rooftop.'

—

Who? Danny Vermeer, project manager for Van Agtmaal BV contractors
Where? Wilhelminakade
On the roof since? 2015
What? (Long stay) hotel rooms, conference halls, rooftop terraces

'The views from the rooftop terraces are wonderful'

—

How difficult is it to build on top of the roof of a historic building?

'The biggest challenge was actually in the cellar. The foundations of the building date from 1898. In order to support the weight of the new buildings on the rooftop we had to remove and replace the whole foundation construction. There were 428 piles, thirty metres each, divided into thirty separate one metre sections. We used a small pile driver to drive them between the 125 existing piles into the ground. In order to be able to park cars between them, we had to make the old concrete columns thinner. It was an exciting six months in which nothing was achieved that was visible to the outside world.'

Why build a hotel rather than apartments on top of the building?

'Van Agtmaal's original idea was indeed to construct apartments. But there is a huge demand for places to sleep in hip and happening Rotterdam and there is a

shortage of hotels in the city. That is why, five years ago, we elected to build a 217 room four storey hotel.'

If there is so much demand for hotel rooms, why only build two storeys on the rooftop rather than for example ten or more?

'The design of this building had to fit in with the city council's plans for the Wilhelminapier. That is: high-rise at the edges, with a central core of authentic low-rise buildings. That was fine for us. We liked the idea of managing an old building and so have chosen for preservation in combination with new construction.'

How was the design received?

'It took years before we could get started. Several surveys, investigations and inspections were carried out before the design was eventually finalised. It also took a long time for the building inspectors to grant the necessary licences and permits.

Once the licenses were finally in order, we contacted the Spanish hotel chain Room Mate Hotels.

After six years of renovation and new construction, our work was completed last autumn. The Spanish architect Teresa Sapey furnished the hotel. She was also responsible for the design of the Room Mate Hotels in Barcelona and Pau.

Room Mate Hotel wanted a jacuzzi on the communal rooftop terrace for the hotel guests.

'They have jacuzzis in their other hotels. However, we advised against this here. How many days a year in the Netherlands can you actually use this? On the communal rooftop terrace on the 5th floor on the Las Palmas side there is space for an outdoor bar. In good weather this can be rolled out onto the terrace. Furthermore, there are rooftop terraces at all corners of the building providing wonderful views on all sides. The architect has done a fantastic job.'

Laurensveste

For many years now, it has been possible to play tennis on the rooftop of the Laurensveste housing complex in the Hoogkwartier district. The complex, designed by Hoogstad Weeber Schulze & Van Tilburg architects, was built in 1985 on one of the last remaining undeveloped wasteland areas within the so-called fire boundary – the periphery of the Second World War bombardment of Rotterdam on the 14th of May, 1940. A multi-storey car park on the Kipstraat sits between the three residential blocks. Three tennis courts have been constructed on the rooftop of this car park. Access is via the walkway from the apartments or via steps from the Hoogstraat. The tennis courts belong to MyGym health club whose members may freely use the courts. The courts may be hired by non-members.

YELLOW ROOFS

HENRI BONTENBAL, STRATEGIST FOR STEDIN
THE EFFECT OF THE GROWING NUMBER OF SOLAR ENERGY ROOFTOPS

'How to directly use the electricity generated by your rooftop solar panels'

According to Stedin, in 2017, there were 90,000 m² of solar panels on the rooftops of Rotterdam. The network operator responsible for the electricity network in the Randstad, the most urbanized area of the Netherlands, predicts that this figure will steadily increase. Stedin's strategist Henri Bontebal studies technological developments in the energy sector. 'Rooftops are going to play an important role in making the Netherlands more sustainable. After all, rooftops are a potential source of energy. The good news is that more and more households and businesses are starting to utilize this potential.'

The solar power that is generated on the rooftops directly affects the underground electricity network. Henri is keeping a close watch on the unprecedented increase in the number of solar panels on household rooftops. 'Four houses in my street have solar panels on their roofs. If, on sunny summer days, these generate a lot of electricity, the surplus goes to the neighbours. But if in some districts there are too many solar panels on the roofs, then the electricity network can become overloaded.' This is not yet the case, but Stedin hopes to avoid the necessity of having to significantly upgrade its electricity network. 'After all, we use public money to manage the electricity network, so any extra maintenance costs are ultimately paid for by the general public.'

'We need to avoid using electricity during peak time on the net"

—

Stylish

Do not misunderstand him. Henri is delighted with every individual rooftop owner who decides to harness solar energy. 'Stedin firmly supports the agreements for CO_2 reductions laid down in the Paris Climate Accord. Renewable energy generation is definitely needed if these agreements are to be met. Rooftops – both flat and sloping – are ideal places for the generation of solar power. More and more home owners are prepared to invest in solar rooftops and solar panels are becoming ever cheaper. Five years ago, I paid about € 6,000 for my solar panels, now they would cost only half that. Furthermore, aesthetics is no longer a reason to install panels only on rooftops in the harbour or on industrial premises; solar panels are becoming increasingly stylish.'

Smart

Care must be taken to ensure that, in the long term, the electricity net does not become overloaded with surplus electricity from solar energy. Henri is looking into innovative ways of using such electricity in households themselves. 'We need to avoid using electricity during peak times. Electricity usage peaks in the morning when the Netherlands awakes and then again in the evening as we cook and watch television. Our first request is for households to use less electricity during these peak times. For example, by charging the electric boiler (high energy consumption) at non-peak times, when there is a surplus of electricity from solar energy. In the near future, electricity providers will be able to advise about such "smart charging". This spread of electricity usage throughout the day prevents "build ups" in the network.'

Battery

On average, 80% of the energy used in households comes from natural gas and 20% from electricity. On sunny days, solar panels can generate much more electricity than this 20%. Stedin is looking to use electric car batteries to temporarily store the surplus. 'More and more electric cars are coming onto the streets, but for 90% of the time they stand still. You can easily use them to power a household. And you don't need to worry that the battery will be low when you need the car. A smart app will ensure that it is ready and charged.'

ALICE KREKT, PROGRAM MANAGER DELTALINQS ENERGY FORUM
COLLECTIVE SOLAR ROOFTOPS IN THE PORT

'The port has 200,000 m² of rooftops waiting to be used'

CO₂ emissions in the Netherlands must be drastically reduced if the environmental agreements laid down in the Paris climate accord are to be met. One fifth of these emissions are produced by the port of Rotterdam. According to program manager Alice Krekt from Deltalinqs Energy Forum, the solution could lie on the rooftops. 'An initial analysis indicates there are 200,000 m² of potentially suitable rooftops. These could support 120,000 solar panels generating renewable electricity for eight thousand households.'

Deltalinqs represents about seven hundred companies in the port. These companies, together with Rotterdam City Council, the Province of South Holland and the Port of Rotterdam, have set up the Deltalinqs Energy Forum to increase the sustainability and resilience of the port area. 'Production processes and transport in the port require a lot of energy. The current era of fossil fuel energy is coming to an end; the next, transition, phase is expected to last twenty to thirty years. The Port of Rotterdam aims to be at the international forefront of this energy transition and is investing in renewable energy forms: wind, biofuels, geothermal and solar.'

Growth

In 2020, the Netherlands would like 14% of its energy consumption to be renewable. To achieve this, as many rooftops as possible must be used to generate electricity from solar energy. The capacity for generating electricity from solar energy in the port has increased from 0.9 megawatt in 2015 to 1.68 megawatt in 2016. 'This growth is mainly due to the installation of 7,500 m² of solar panels at FrigoCare (see page 180), an open transhipment company for refrigerated and frozen products in the Waalhaven. The biggest potential for further increasing the area of solar rooftops would appear to be the distribution ports Waalhaven, Botlek and on the first Maasvlakte.

Alice is responsible for bundling the rooftops belonging to various companies. 'A rooftop of 1,000 m² is not big enough to interest solar power providers; lease contracts are ideally given for rooftops larger than 3,500 m². By collectively combining rooftops, businesses can together create the required mass.'

The solar power provider takes responsibility

The advantage of a collective contract is that the solar power provider takes complete responsibility: the businesses themselves do not have to worry about it. 'That is important because, while the businesses would like the port to become sustainable, energy transition is not their core business. They need to concentrate on their primary processes but do realise that energy transition is the way to go, that CO₂ emissions must be reduced, that sustainable techniques can be profitable and that solar power is good for the environment.'

Tipping point

Alice supports companies in their search for the best solution for them. They discuss revenue models – investing, leasing or other options – as well as exploitation and maintenance. For the collective construction, costs are usually recovered within seven to nine years. 'In October 2018, we would like to collectively submit an application for a substantial subsidy, so that we can start work on harnessing the sun's energy in the port as soon as possible.' Waiting a few more years for a technical breakthrough or further progress – such as solar cells with mega capacity – is not an option. 'It will be a while before new, better and more efficient techniques are available and affordable. We are now at the tipping point and need to set to work straight away. The businesses who dare take steps now, will smooth the way for those who follow.'

'Collective rooftops for harnessing solar energy'

***

Noorderhavenkade

Commissioned by: Blijstroom

Existing building: a gym

Number of solar panels: 183

Electricity generated: 45,750 kilowatt hours guaranteed per year

Distribution area: post codes 3011, 3013, 3031, 3032, 3033, 3035, 3037, 3038, 3039

Access: via steps on the side of the sports hall

Construction period: May-June 2017

Contractor: Switch Energy

An idealist's rooftop hunt

Energy corporation Blijstroom's aim is for Rotterdam to become energy neutral by 2027. To achieve this, volunteer Julia Hevemeyer approaches owners of large, vacant city rooftops to ask whether she may install solar panels on their roofs. 'Now, four years after we started, our first collective solar rooftop supplies electricity to 57 neighbouring apartments. Additional solar rooftops are in the pipeline.'

Who? Julia Hevemeyer, Blijstroom volunteer
Where? Noorderhavenkade
On the roof since? 2017
What? Solar panels

Over the next ten years, Blijstroom hopes to create as many collective solar rooftops as possible in the city.

'Our dream is that in ten years' time, Rotterdam will be able to generate enough renewable electricity to be 100% self-sufficient. We are starting with electricity from rooftop solar panels because this technology has already been tried and tested.'

Solar power is a hot topic in Rotterdam, according to network provider Stedin, last autumn.

'Sustainability is hot, and about time too. For the last twenty years, Blijstroom volunteers have been saying that we need to reduce our reliance on fossil fuels. Generating clean energy is good for Rotterdam, good for your wallet and good for the world.'

Why is Blijstroom concentrating on collective solar rooftops rather than on individual rooftops?

'It turns out that harnessing solar energy on your own rooftop is not as simple as you would imagine. Small, private rooftops are not big enough to install enough solar panels to generate sufficient electricity, or they do not face the sun, or they are owned by someone else. The electricity that Blijstroom generates is offered to the people of Rotterdam who do not have their own suitable rooftop. And to tenants in rental houses.'

How does Blijstroom find suitable rooftops?

'We look for large, vacant rooftops in the city. School buildings, sports halls, home owners' associations, office complexes, club buildings and tram depots for example. All of these could become suitable solar rooftops. We then ask the owners for permission to use their rooftops.'

Are owners prepared to lend you their rooftops?

'Yes. Rotterdam City Council donated our first solar rooftop - the Noorderhavenkade gym in Blijdorp. Since solar panels were installed last spring, the roof has supplied electricity to 57 consumers. The city council supports our initiative because solar power contributes to reducing CO_2 and fine dust particle emissions. Our second rooftop, in the Liskwartier District, is from SKAR, Foundation for Artists' Accommodation in Rotterdam. Roof three in Bospolder-Tussendijken is another rooftop belonging to the city council. We are going to set up a pilot there, to see whether we can make a business case for solar panels for people on a limited budget.'

Blijstroom is a non-profit organisation run by volunteers.

'That's right. Our challenge is to grow from a cooperative initiative to a provider of renewable electricity. We will need to become more professional. But I believe it is possible to be both idealistic and run a profitable business.'

How can the people of Rotterdam purchase the electricity from your solar rooftops?

'By becoming a member of our corporation, by investing in the solar panel sections and by purchasing electricity from Qurrent, our partner. Qurrent will then offset the solar electricity generated by us with your energy bill. We guarantee that your investment will be recovered with interest.'

FrigoCare

The largest solar park in Rotterdam is located on the 7,500 m² rooftop of FrigoCare's freezer warehouse in the Waalhaven (see page 176). This park has 3,100 solar panels that annually generate 750,000 kilowatt-hours of electricity. This is enough to meet one third of the warehouse's electricity requirements.

The solar park is a joint venture between FrigoCare, Zon Exploitatie Nederland (ZEN) and the Port of Rotterdam.

FrigoCare invested € 650,000 in renovating the roof. ZEN paid € 1 million and is responsible for exploitation and maintenance of the solar park. It is expected that these costs will be recovered within ten years. The collaboration with ZEN reduces FrigoCare's annual CO_2 emissions by about 325 tonnes, enough to provide 250 families with electricity for a whole year.

Hooidrift

In the Randstad, the most urbanized area of the Netherlands, the number of rooftops with solar panels is steadily increasing. Each month, one thousand new solar rooftops are registered. Rotterdam now generates 11.1 megawatt of electricity from solar panels; more than any other city in the Netherlands except for Utrecht, Amersfoort and The Hague. According to network provider Stedin (see page 174), the growth is explained by the fact that solar panels are becoming ever better and ever cheaper. The good economic climate in the Netherlands is also encouraging more rooftop owners to invest.

In the first half of 2017, the Randstad's solar rooftop capacity increased by 25% compared to the same period last year. These solar panels generate enough renewable electricity to power 87,000 households for a whole year.

The photo shows private solar rooftops on the Hooidrift. The owners of the fifth rooftop from the right have chosen to create a mini rooftop farm (see page 78).

183

First Rotterdam

The First Rotterdam office block, opposite the Groot Handelsgebouw (see page 122) with The Suicide Club (see page 152) on the top corner, has been awarded the BREEAM sustainability label 'excellent'. This means that the building's sustainability score is an average of 70% to 85%.

The more than 160 solar panels on its various rooftops helped First Rotterdam earn this certificate. These enable the building to generate enough electricity to meet most of its own requirements.

The fifty panels on the green sedum rooftop of the 128-metre-high tower are the highest solar panels in the Netherlands. Another green rooftop provides shelter for bats and peregrine falcons. Rainwater on the rooftops is collected and used in a grey water system for flushing toilets.

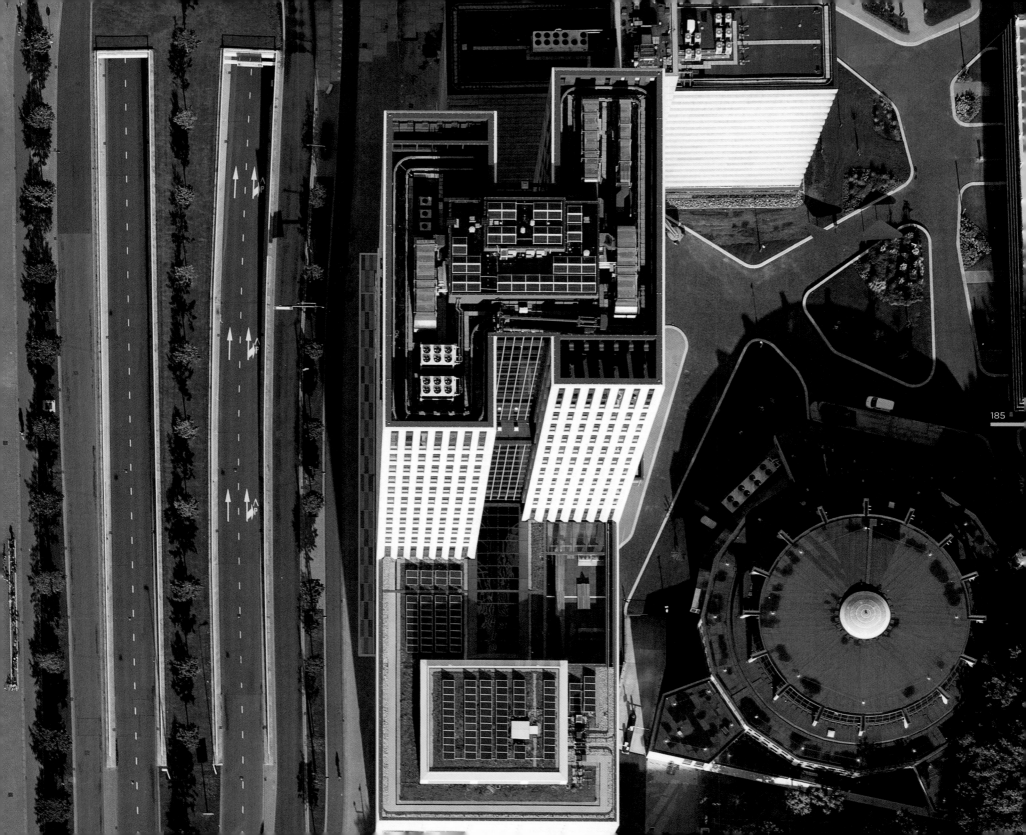

GLIMPSE OF
THE FUTURE

187

HOFBOGEN GREEN PROMENADE, A NATURAL CITY IDEA

'Developing rooftops is a specific skill'

The Rotterdam University of Applied Science's (elective) "multifunctional rooftops" course fits in with current rooftop trends. Last school year, the new course was successfully tested in cooperation with the Schieland and de Krimpenerwaard Water Authorities and the Rotterdam City Council. Since September 2017, it has been included as an official course for first and second year students. 'There are many issues concerning the construction of roofs and our students should be able to help.'

Kaj van de Sandt from the university's Department for Water Management coordinates the practical projects and the elective multifunctional rooftops course. 'Our basic principle is that students become better professionals if they work on real life topics.' The University has defined five areas of experimentation within which students and university lecturers work together with professionals on topics related to the course, the professional field and the city. Kaj's work involves experiments in the City Centre. 'We have identified some interesting case studies for the rooftops in the city.

Discussions with the water authorities (see page 36) and the city council have led to a range of real life projects for students of all levels.'

'Our students are able to contribute to the development of the city'

—

Enthusiastic

Last school year, a number of third year students worked on a six month project in the Agniese Neighbourhood, near the Hofbogen. 'They analysed the suitability and use of flat rooftops for rainwater collection and presented it in comic book form. This was such a success that they have been invited to residents' meetings. Such recognition is extremely encouraging for the students.'

First and second year students following the elective course multifunctional rooftops have discussed case studies of the Bijenkorf (see page 142) and 7 Square Endeavour (see page 199). The latter project concerns the development of rooftops around the Schouwburgplein. 'The most interesting idea they devised for the Bijenkorf, was a catwalk for fashion shows. For 7 Square Endeavour, the students visited the residential towers to ask what people wanted to do with their rooftops. Everyone was enthusiastic. In all cases, our students were able to make a real contribution to the development of the city. And, it turns out that students work harder when they feel that their ideas are appreciated.'

Attractive

Most students taking part in the practical projects were from the water management, urban and special planning and real estate departments. The elective course multifunctional rooftops mainly attracted civil engineering students; although students from water management, geography, spatial planning and even nursing were also interested. 'We want to make the rooftop subjects attractive to as wide a range of students as possible.'

On practical projects and in the lessons, a mix of students from various disciplines actively work together on assignments. 'It is very important that the students learn to work together. That they learn right from the start that in a complex urban environment such as Rotterdam, they will not get far if they only approach things from their own discipline. A civil engineering student must learn that the world is much more than a calculation of the stress forces on a rooftop. For the success of a project, other aspects, such as legal, policy, financial and social issues, are just as important.'

Perfect preparation

Kaj's ultimate aim is to ensure that the students graduate and become the new professionals in the city. 'Time and again, we see that our experimental setup is an excellent preparation for the students' future. It really has an effect on a student when a professional asks: "Have you considered this?" Much more than when we, as lecturers, ask.'

MARIT HAAKSMA, ROOFTOP GRADUATE
THE ADDED VALUE OF COMBINING ROOFTOPS

'Linking rooftops increases their usefulness and value'

Marit Haaksma is one of the new generation of urban developers. She graduated from Delft University of Technology in June 2017 with her master's thesis on Rotterdam's rooftops. 'Graduate studies do not have to concern themselves with reality. The focus can be on visionary ideas. My idea is: attract people to the rooftops and link the rooftops together. This leads to the ultimate combination of compacting, greening and connecting. Given the right structure, the roofscape will grow organically.'

In her master's project *Roof Structure Rotterdam: designing the fifth facade of the city centre in Rotterdam*, Marit considers public space to be the core of the roofscape. 'The realisation that rooftops are frequently only viewed from ground level was a revelation. By looking at rooftops from other angles, down from the ever increasing number of high-rise buildings and sideways from neighbouring rooftops, you actually get a 3D view of them: from below, from above and from the side.'

Soaring

A horizontal city is a city that spreads outwards towards the outskirts. A vertical city grows upward. In Marit's thesis she presents a new phenomenon: a diagonal city with rooftops on which functions and activities can be combined. 'The current architectural concept is: I have a building, this has a roof, what should I do with it? The value of rooftops can be greatly increased if they are linked: a green roof is just one green roof; however, a series of green rooftops can become a park with a rainwater pool in which children can play. By designing in this fashion, the rooftops form a new element, contributing unique new qualities to the city that cannot be found at ground level: space, peace and quiet, green areas, water storage and promenades. Places where people can literally and figuratively soar above the bustling city.'

Savanna theory

During her own research, Marit discovered that very few studies concerning people on rooftops have been carried out. But, what information she did find, is promising. 'Psychology research suggests that we are biologically attracted to high places. This is the Savannah theory, derived from our nomadic ancestors in the savanna, who continually moved to new areas in the search for food. They chose safer high lying places, from where they could easily survey the surroundings. It seems to me that this behaviour is still inborn because, one way or another, we always want to go upwards. In an unfamiliar city, people are attracted to church towers or lookout points. Going on to a rooftop is a real experience. Just look at the popularity of the Rotterdam Rooftop Days (see page 14) and last year's temporary stairs (see page 126) to the roof of the Groot Handelsgebouw (see page 122).'

Accessible

If the rooftops in Rotterdam's city centre are to become open to the public, they

'The rooftops can become places where people literally and figuratively soar above the bustling city'

—

must be made accessible from the streets. Marit's suggestions for this include stairs and lifts going up and down as well as promenades. 'The so-called Rotterdam level in the city centre at a height of about 25 metres is perfect for this. You can also make use of existing architecture: the beautiful stairwells of the Lijnbaan flats (see page 194) already provide vertical connections. I would imagine that building a bridge to the Lijnbaan wouldn't be too difficult.'

Three perspectives

Marit has drawn three perspectives of the future city as experienced by: a resident in a high-rise building, a tourist and the shopping public.

High-rise resident

In Marit's design, if you live above the Rotterdam layer (8th floor), you could choose to go to the 10th floor instead of down to ground level. There you find rooftop walking routes, which take you to work or to the supermarket. The alternative, current situation, is to go down to ground level, and involves going in and out of buildings and up and down.

Tourist

From Central Station (see page 48), a tourist can stroll all the way to Markthal via rooftop promenades. From this height, all the prominent buildings in the city can be seen. It is easy to find your way and there are beautiful views of the skyline.

Shopping public

Pausing between shops, you can go up to a rooftop to relax on a bench and enjoy the view. In other cities, it is quite common to buy bread and cheese and eat your lunch on a park bench. In the centre of Rotterdam, there are currently few suitable places to relax free of charge. The rooftops address this issue.

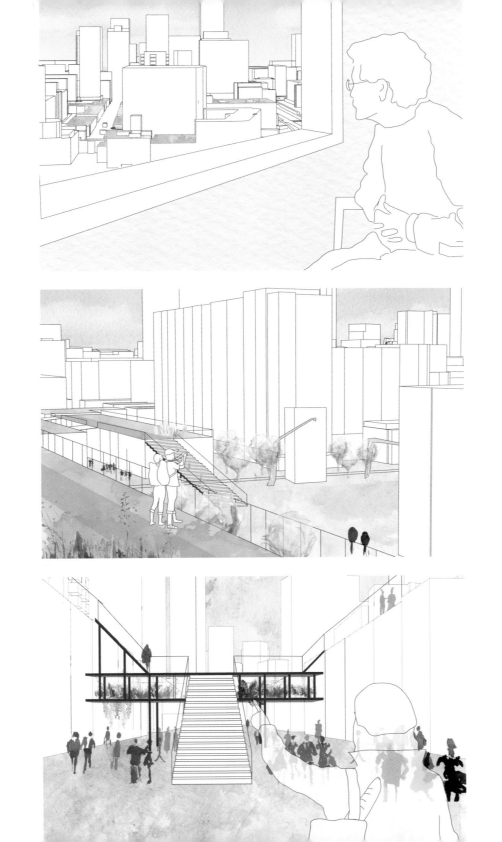

Karel's Cafe, Clubhouse & Roofgarden

Members will be able to take the lift from the central hall and from the first floor Clubhouse to the 13th floor rooftop garden. The rooftop garden will encompass the whole 1100 m² of the Lijnbaan flats. From left to right the following amenities will be created: Karel's rooftop cafe and bar, a restaurant with a terrace and a rooftop garden with an orangery for workshops and private dining. The terrace will be suitable for yoga lessons, personal training and film evenings. Karel's Cafe and Clubhouse are expected to be completed by the end of 2018. The rooftop garden should be ready for use in 2019.

A rooftop garden as part of a total concept

Who? Steven Manhave, owner of Manhave Vastgoed
Where? Corner of the Kruiskade and the Karel Doormanstraat
On the roof since? 2018/2019
What? Karel's Clubhouse & Rooftop Garden

———

In 2018-2019, the owner of Manhave Real Estate intends to create a ground floor cafe-brasserie and first floor members only clubhouse with access to a 1100 m² rooftop garden, in and on the Lijnbaan Flats (City House) on the corner of the Kruiskade and the Karel Doormanstraat. Steven Manhave: 'We are creating a special place here where people can meet each other, relax and seek inspiration. The rooftop garden is part of this concept.'

It all started two and a half years ago with the idea of creating an outdoor area for the residents of City House.

'We were devising long term plans for living, working and shopping in the area. Initially the rooftop garden was indeed intended for the residents of City House. We would like this to remain a pleasant and safe neighbourhood with good social cohesion. An inspirational meeting place is an essential part of such a neighbourhood and there simply is no such place in the city centre. The rooftop seemed to be the perfect place to create such a meeting place. The design team consists of ZZDP Architects from Amsterdam and Studio Ilse from London.

At what point did the roof become part of a total concept?

'The roof became part of the total concept when we started working with Ilse Crawford, the renowned London designer and creative director.' We had approached Ilse because, like us, she has a people-centred approach. Ilse excels in creating that "homely feeling" that we wanted for the neighbourhood. This is the first time that Ilse has worked in the Netherlands.'

Ilse's design extends much further than just the rooftop

'She creates an environment in which you really can relax. Not just a home, but much more.'

Which trends do you hope to cater for with this concept?

'The increase in the number of single person households and urban nomads. The cafe-brasserie Karel's will be open from early morning to late at night. The people of Rotterdam, day trippers and tourists can come there to meet each other, have a bite to eat or get a take-away. The members only Clubhouse hopes to provide a solution for the increasing need of belonging to a community: like-minded people enjoy meeting each other in a safe and inspiring setting. We will provide valet parking as well as car and bicycle sharing. This helps limit traffic in the city centre and contributes to a sustainable, resilient city.'

There are many shops skirting the Lijnbaan flats. Do you actively follow developments in the retail industry?

'Absolutely. The retail industry is much more dynamic than it used to be. What is hip now, will no longer be so in three years' time. We need to be flexible and take this into account. Ilse helped with advice about the choice of shops. These will be a mix of international and national local heroes. All of them retailers with passion for their trade.'

Does this mean the end of the Kruiskade as the most fashionable shopping street in Rotterdam?

'That is not how we see ourselves. We hope to provide a diverse mix of shops and amenities. We are working to improve the soul of the city because we love Rotterdam. There is a reason that our slogan is *Love the city*. This new concept has given us another slogan: *We dare to go beyond*.'

Karel's Clubhouse & Rooftop Garden

The exclusive, first floor members only clubhouse will open towards the end of 2018 and will have its own separate entrance on the Kruiskade. A hospitality manager will welcome members and provide valet parking and tickets for shows etc. There will be a cocktail bar, restaurant and a special kitchen where cooking workshops can be held. Members can come to Karel's Clubhouse to work, participate in workshops and hire rooms for private or business events. A fitness studio and Skins Cosmetics beauty salon will be among the facilities. A lift from the clubhouse provides easy access to the rooftop garden on the 13th floor.

196

Karel's Cafe

Karel's street level cafe-brasserie with terrace is scheduled to open towards the end of 2018. It is intended to be a home-from-home, open for breakfast, lunch, drinks and dinner from 07:00 until 01:00. The chef will also provide takeaway sandwiches, cakes and evening meals. For day trippers and tourists, it will be a convenient meeting place near Central Station from where they can easily go shopping and to where they can return for drinks and dinner. Purchases can be temporarily stored in lockers while visitors go to the cinema or a show. Valet parking is available for additional ease of use.

197

Hofbogen

Many ideas have been presented for the nearly two kilometres long Hofbogen (railway arches) rooftop. One of these is The Urbanist's Aqueduct 010, commissioned by the city council's Water Sensitive Rotterdam. In this design, the rooftop of the historic Hofplein line is adapted to collect, transport and purify rainwater that is then recycled. The plan includes green spaces and play areas as well as promenades where people can stroll and relax.

The Hofbogen rooftop (see page 146) is owned in part by ProRail and in part by the Hofbogen Foundation. The city council has right of use. The Hofbogen, including the roof, are expected to be sold within about eighteen months. Only then will it become clear exactly which plans for the rooftop will actually be carried out.

Sustainable
housing along the
former Hofplein
railway

Children's water
playground

Neighbourhood
laundrette

New swimming
pool in the district
Rotterdam North

Local
brewers

7 Square Endeavour

7 Square Endeavour is an initiative set up by several parties including Theatre Rotterdam, Arcadis, the Doelen, Dura Vermeer, Eneco, the Schieland and Krimpenerwaard Water Authorities, the ministry of Infrastructure and the Environment and TNO. A survey carried out by this initiative has shown that a number of roofs around the Schouwburgplein will need to be replaced within the coming five years. 7 Square Endeavour's mission is to make the Schouwburgplein resilient and ensure that it remains a pleasant place to live. One way of doing this is to create multifunctional rooftops round the square. Well-known buildings in this district include the Doelen, Codarts, Pathé, Calypso and the Pauluskerk. In 2018, Manhave Real Estate will be the first to make a start, with their rooftop project on City House (the Lijnbaan Flats) on the Kruiskade (see page 194).

Depot

A public rooftop park will be constructed 41 metres above the ground, on top of the new Depot for Boijmans van Beuningen's museum. Architectural firm MVRDV (see page 138) has designed the shining building in Museum Park to display the museum depot's treasures and make them accessible to everyone. An art route will zigzag from the ground floor reception through the building, upwards to the green rooftop garden with its exhibition space, restaurant and sculpture garden. The rooftop, with its panoramic views of Museum Park and the Rotterdam skyline, will be protected all round by a windbreak. Construction started in March 2017 and the Depot and the public park are expected to be open to the general public from 2019.

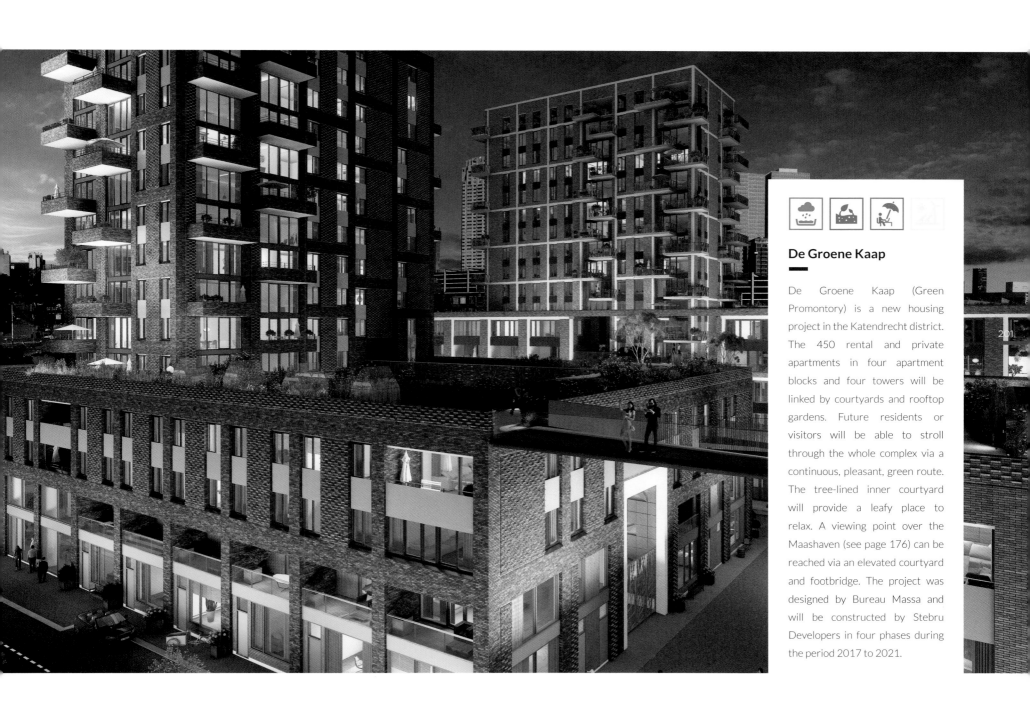

De Groene Kaap

De Groene Kaap (Green Promontory) is a new housing project in the Katendrecht district. The 450 rental and private apartments in four apartment blocks and four towers will be linked by courtyards and rooftop gardens. Future residents or visitors will be able to stroll through the whole complex via a continuous, pleasant, green route. The tree-lined inner courtyard will provide a leafy place to relax. A viewing point over the Maashaven (see page 176) can be reached via an elevated courtyard and footbridge. The project was designed by Bureau Massa and will be constructed by Stebru Developers in four phases during the period 2017 to 2021.

Robert Fruinstraat

The Robert Fruinstraat is an 'ordinary' street in the Middelland neighbourhood, in between the city centre and the Delfshaven district. The sewerage system, gas infrastructure and electricity grid in this street all need replacing, which makes this an ideal opportunity to implement change. With the help of residents, businesses and local institutions in the street, the Municipality is currently redesigning the street. Key values for the development of a resilient street are water retention, sustainability, collaboration and value creation. Green roofs and an innovative 'urban water buffer' are integral parts of the new design.

Green roof

Solar panels

Polder roof

Roof garden

Rain water use in the street

Urban Water Buffer

Tiny Houses

The large-scale construction of green roofs is happening much too slowly for Studio Walden. The main reason for this, according to the design agency, is that investments are not financially viable. Their solution: combine green rooftops with rooftop villages or environmentally friendly 'tiny houses'. Rooftop owners recover their investments by letting or selling the houses. The residents have an exciting place to live and look after the green 'garden'. A win-win situation all round.

To promote this rooftop lifestyle, Noortje Veerman and Jan-Willem van der Male's tiny house (from Tiny House Rotterdam) was moved to the rooftop of the Gele Gebouw (Yellow Building) on the Zomerhofstraat for five days and nights during the Rotterdam Rooftop Days 2017 (see page 136 and 140). Studio Walden are looking for suitable rooftops to further experiment with this concept.

De Heuvel

Over the coming five years, with the aid of a European LIFE-program subsidy (see page 20), Rotterdam City Council will develop a number of rooftops in the city. One of these is on the municipal post-war building known as De Heuvel (The Hill) on the Grotekerkplein, the site, with its statue of Erasmus, that has traditionally been a centre for debate and discussion. De Heuvel will become a model for the resilient, multifunctional development of rooftops in the city. The four rooftops will each have their own 'colour': an energy rooftop with solar panels (yellow); a social rooftop with rooftop bar (red); a rooftop garden (green); and a rooftop pond with water plants (blue). All four rooftops will be open to the general public.

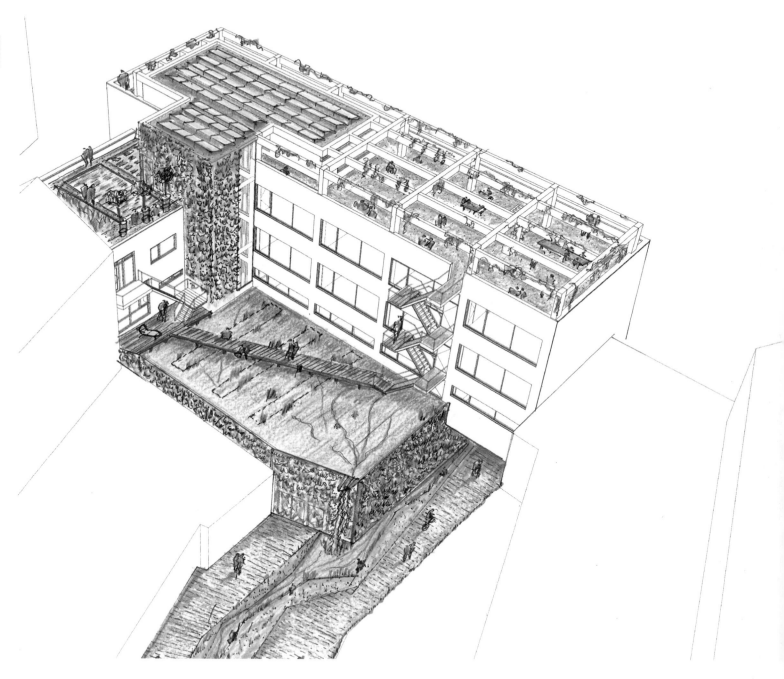

Fenix 1

The Fenix warehouses on the Rijnhaven date from 1922. They were originally constructed for the Holland America Line. On the rooftop of Fenix Warehouse 1 – left of the Rijnhaven bridge as seen from Hotel New York – 212 lofts will be constructed following a design by Mei architects and planners. The first storey on top of the historic foundations will surround a 2000 m² communal rooftop garden.

The Rijnhaven side will be taller, with more storeys, so that visually the building will slope down to the Deliplein. Internally, the lofts can be divided vertically and horizontally, as required, and all lofts will have a rooftop terrace or balcony. The warehouse itself will become Fenix Docks, home to dance company Conny Janssen Danst, Codarts university of the arts and Circus Rotjeknor.

At 45,000 m², this is one of the largest construction projects in the Netherlands. It is expected to be completed in the second quarter of 2019.

The Rotterdam Roofscape

In 2015 the Rotterdam City Council asked De Urbanisten (see page 26) to create an image of the Rotterdam Roofscape with blue, green, red and yellow rooftops. What De Urbanisten's image does not do is to link the rooftops (orange). Dirk van Peijpe: "I am a strong supporter of giving the general public as much space as possible at street level. I do not think that such connected structures at a great height are interesting or attractive. Why would you want to link the rooftop of the Groot Handelsgebouw to the rooftop of the Doelen concert hall? It is much more interesting to know that the Doelen will have a wonderful rooftop where you can relax before or after a concert, or as far as I am concerned, even when there is no concert. And then you cross the Schouwburgplein, via the Kruisplein – which forms a pleasant route over the newly designed Stationsplein – to the Groot Handelsgebouw and Central Station. In this way, you enjoy an architectural walk through interesting streets.' (See also pages 20, 90 and 190)

Historic buildings, too, provide opportunities for creating resilient rooftops

High rooftops provide space for seclusion and concentration, views and contemplation

High rooftops promote biodiversity; they are unreachable and provide vantage points for predators and shelter for prey

High rooftops are places for partying and entertainment with the city centre as a backdrop

An energy landscape traces the urban composition of the typical post-war districts

There is space for large-scale solar farms on the rooftops of warehouses in the port areas

High rooftops catch the wind, especially when they face west

Urban farming can give sturdy rooftops a new lease on life

Large car park rooftops are spacious enough for sport roofscapes

The 19th century block of buildings forms a multi-coloured, intensively used roofscape

The asphalted, logistical port environment provides opportunities for large-scale rooftop ecology

Public rooftop parks will enrich large commercial buildings

Aesthetically pleasing rooftop gardens contrast with the rugged decor of the city centre

The blue rooftop reflects the ever changing Rotterdam sky

Suburban streets have efficient roofscapes

Acknowledgements

This book would not have been possible without the trust and enthusiastic support of the more than 150 people involved.

My sincere thanks go to the many sponsors, interviewees, producers and advisers.

I would like to extend a special thank you to Marcel Jongmans (Inspirationalist, idea for the book); Paul van Roosmalen and Eveline Bronsdijk (Rotterdam City Council, my rocks and shoulders to cry on); Joep Klabbers and Léon van Geest (Rotterdam Rooftop Days, for their help and support in selecting example rooftops); Dirk van Peijpe (De Urbanisten, for the structure and organisation in functional colours); Marieke Odekerken, Chris Bonis and Ossip van Duivenbode (for the wonderful photographs); Martin Hanning (Rotterdam City Council, for his historical research); Sigrid Schenk (Rebel, for her business case reflection); Frans Happel (journalist and writer, for his critical proof reading); Wim van der Lee (for the detailed text correction); Arjen van Riel and Jenny Spierenburg-Zaagman (carenza*, for the attractive style and design) and Veenman+ (for the printing).

In addition, I would also like to thank my advisers: Koen Voskamp (finance); Katja Verdoorn (project management); Margot Bleeker, Ellis van den Berg, Margriet Jansen and Jocelyn Rebbens (sponsoring) and Marieke Odekerken and Micheline van Neste (overall sounding boards).

Thanks also to Marcel Witvoet and Janine van den Dool (nai010 publishers, for final advice concerning editing, design and PR of the Dutch version of the book: Het Rotterdamse Dakenboek, nieuw gebruik van dak en stad)

Furthermore, I am most grateful to my family and friends who have supported and helped me.

Sponsors

www.rotterdam.nl/groenedaken

www.multifunctioneledaken.nl

www.rotterdam.nl/wonen-leven/urban-roofs

www.zoontjens.nl

www.binder.nl

www.hhsk.nl

www.stedin.net

www.manhave.com

Colophon

Author
Esther Wienese

English translation
Rachael Fox (Fennec Vertalingen)
Anne Wolfson

Concept
Esther Wienese
Marcel Jongmans
Marieke Odekerken
Arjen van Riel

Project manager and producer
Esther Wienese

Sponsor recruitment
Esther Wienese

Text contributions
Martin Hanning – history
Sigrid Schenk – business case

Final editing and correction
Frans Happel
Wim van der Lee
Marcel Witvoet

Design
carenza*

Printing
Veenman+

Photographs
Chris Bonis – panorama photos and photo page 67
Ossip van Duivenbode – cover, aerial photos and photos on pages 111, 113, 126, 146, 151 and 212
Marieke Odekerken – portraits of the visionaries and the photos on pages 8, 32, 50, 59, 74, 77, 78, 81, 88, 97, 101, 104, 131, 132, 134, 135, 152, 155 top, 159, 166, 169 and 211
Arnoud Voet – historical photos
Peter Schmidt – photo page 38
Alain Gil Gonzales – photo page 87
Frank Hanswijk – photos pages 140, 172 and 178
Sander Stoepker – photo page 145
The Suicide Club – photo page 155 bottom
Rutger van der Zwaag / Maurits Falkena, Silver Motion Pictures – photo page 163

De Natuurlijke Stad – artist's impression page 186
Marit Haaksma – artist's impressions page 193
ZZDP Architecten – artist's impressions page 194, 196 and 197
De Urbanisten – artist's impressions page 198, 206 and 207
Arcadis – artist's impression page 199
MVRDV – artist's impression page 200
Het Nieuwe Concept – artist's impression page 201
Martijn Bakker, Gemeente Rotterdam – artist's impression page 202
Studio Walden – artist's impression page 203
LG architecten – artist's impression page 204
Mei & WAX – artist's impression page 205

Distribution
Esther Wienese
www.estherwienese.nl
©Esther Wienese

ISBN 978-90-828610-0-6

**'Everything I love
is on the rooftops:
Rotterdam, people, views,
water, nature, energy,
architecture, life, work,
relaxation and innovation'**

—

About the author

Esther Wienese (1965) is a writer and Rotterdam guide. Since 2006, she has engaged with the city she so loves: asking questions, writing, telling narratives and connecting. Esther specialises in writing narratives based on interviews. By asking and continuing to ask questions she is able to explain abstract topics in concrete, accessible and human terms. As guide, she narrates stories in and about the city.

For *Rotterdam Rooftops*, Esther interviewed about fifty roofing experts and rooftop owners in their own environments. She attracted sponsors, produced the book and launched it during the Rotterdam City Centre Symposium 2017 with its Rooftop theme. Esther also produced this English translation to internationally promote Rotterdam as model city.

Esther has written about water and innovative urban developments for amongst others the Rotterdam City Council, Rotterdam Partners and various local magazines. In addition, she is an enthusiastic and talented story teller. For "Rotterdam Tours" and "Inside Rotterdam" she guided visitors around the Markthal, The Rotterdam, the Timmerhuis, the city centre and the harbour. From that experiences she now organises guided tours of the rooftops of Rotterdam and gives compelling talks about them.

Esther studied at the Utrecht School of Journalism and has worked as business journalist, communications consultant and spokesperson for amongst others KEMA, NS, Room for the River and the National Delta Program.

See also www.estherwienese.nl.

SCHIEBLOCK